# Of God,

# THE DEVIL AND THE JEWS

# Of God,

## The Devil and the Jews

BY

DAGOBERT D. RUNES

**PHILOSOPHICAL LIBRARY**

New York

# Table of Contents

# The Good God and God

## I

ONLY A FEW GENERATIONS AGO, DENIAL OF THE existence of God was in many countries of the Western world punishable by incarceration, even death. And just a few generations further back, denial of the existence of the devil was also considered a capital crime. It stands to reason that only an idea of inherently persuasive power, such as atheism obviously is, would have to be guarded against with such apprehension and ruthlessness. There are no penal threats necessary, for example, against *athanateism* (the disbelief in death) or *avitaism* (the disbelief in life), for there is little concern in the minds of the ruling classes of our society that the people by and large may develop disbelief in the inevitable death of man or disbelief in the inevitable procreation of life by seeding down women or animals or plants.

The existence of God, however, appears to be less obvious to man than the existence of death or of life. And because atheism is a concept that touches almost every man at least once in his life-time, the apprehension in the minds of our rulers is understandable—this atheistic thought, which they consider a denial of one of the primary bases of Western civilization, may become dominant and undermine the minds of the people.

It is a well-known fact that no man is so small that he does not consider himself above the masses. And no matter how humble a personage you approach on matters of a theological nature, he will tell you (unless he is a true believer): "I take no great stock in the gospels, but it's a good thing for the masses." I've yet to find the man or woman who refers to himself as being just part of the masses and who makes an honest statement as to their true needs. The clever but shallow Voltaire once quipped, "If there were no God, it would be necessary to invent Him." It is exactly that attitude, often practiced, which makes the masses, and that means all of us, a bit weary of theologians. The people may believe an unlikely tale if such is repeated and backed by accepted tradition; but in the long run, mere fabrications by the most astute theologians will fail to stem the stream of doubt that comes forth from the minds of the enlightened masses of our time.

I am opening this little discussion on God with remarks about atheism, for the concept of God came late in the life of man. And man lived without God for a million years. He now dwells in the presence of God, but does God dwell in the heart of man?

We must face the fact that not only has man lived for what seems an eternity without God, but at this writing the majority of those who populate our globe still do. The followers of Gautama Buddha, the students of the Veda, the followers of Laotse and Kong Fu-tse—they have no trust in deity. They are confident that Tao teh King (the road to life) is open to them. They can all become Buddhas (enlightened). And there is nothing between them and Nirvana but the weakness of their own flesh and mind.

There are other atheists and agnostics in addition to the philosophizing Asiatics. There are the many who look upon our church life as the woeful remnants of the Dark Ages, in the manner of our anthropologists and ethnologists studying the primitive religions of Australia. There are also other millions in our midst. Some call themselves rationalists; others secularists; most of them don't bother to search for a self-classification.

We must face the fact that the theists are in a minority historically as well as actually. Man can live without God; man can die without God. There is, further, no reason to assume that man without God must necessarily lead a less model life in the social sense than man with God. We must admit that some lives of impeccable conduct were led without a trace of godliness and that some of the most despicable scoundrels ran from pew to pew and from confession to perpetration and back. Any intelligent observer of history must note that religiosity neither includes nor precludes morality— perhaps ideologically, perhaps academically, certainly not historically, and certainly not in human practice. In fact, religiosity in one form or another served as a cloak for the vicious selfish desires of tyrants and other ambitious entrepreneurs. This fact, as well as the fact that theists of the past have on many occasions perpetrated the ugliest of crimes, such as the torture and execution of harmless people because of some point of false belief and superstition, has been often used by atheists as an argument against religion. However, as cruel as these acts were, one cannot rationally base an argument about the existence of God on the misdeeds of confused or corrupt church dignitaries.

We must further face the fact that in all fairness to the pagan world, neither Christians nor Mohammedans, the two dominant God-born religions, have in any appreciable manner contributed to the peace of the world. The Mohammedans when still in power made every effort to convince neighboring countries of their philosophy using scimitar rather than the prayer rug. And since the days of King Constantine, the Christians carried on their proselytizing with a cross that was pointed and deadly at the end. But even among themselves, the awareness of God and His own merciful Son was shadowy, shadowy indeed. The earth of Europe, the earth of the Americas, is drenched with the blood of Christians cut down by Christians, and heathens cut down by Christians, and Jews cut down by Christians—and not for the glory of God but for mere glory and for mere greed.

If we are to believe in God, we cannot base

such a belief on its effect upon the Western world of the last two thousand years. We have done little honor to the Lord in all these years. We broke every commandment but the first one, "Thou shalt have no other God besides me." We shed the blood of the innocent; we allowed our neighbors to starve and perish. And we kept humans as serfs and slaves. We kept Christians like cattle and we used them like cattle. True enough, we kept the first commandment, but this entails nothing but a profession of a fleeting concept. It is easy to say, "I believe in God. I am a Christian." But is God in you? Is Christ in you?

Nowhere is the concept more beautiful than in the Torah of the Hebrews, whence it came to us as well as to the Mohammedans. *Adonai elohainu, adonai echod* (The Eternal is our God, the Eternal is One.) The ancient Hebrews did not write the name of God. I often wish the Christians would follow suit, as never was a word more misused in writing and speaking than the name of the Lord.

The Greeks and Romans used the words "theos" and "deus" with casual ease. They had built up an intricate theistic hierarchy which their artists, poets and writers clothed in a fantastic symbolism.

Basically, the gods of the Greeks and Romans led a stage-and-party life. The people, especially the artists, seemed to follow the gods and goddesses right into their abodes and bedchambers; but the deities rarely came into the life of the Mediterraneans except at public functions and festivals. For the master theologian of that time and period, Plato, God was not only the Idea of Creative Intellect but also the Idea of the Beautiful and the All-Good. Going further, even the souls of the most exalted men became gods in their participation with the god Intellect. This is all very poetic as is the rest of Plato's demonology and polytheistic symbolism. As none of Plato's dialogues lead to final conclusions, his theistic dialogues also leave us in profound obscurity.

The arguments for the existence of God are endless, which itself is an indication that they are neither conclusive nor convincing. Anselm (d. 1109) presented a now classical formulation that God exists because the very idea of a supreme or perfect being requires its existence. Thomas Aquinas (d. 1274) offered five ways of demonstrating God's existence, of which the one deducing a First Cause from secondary causes is widely travelled upon. Immanuel Kant brought in a moral argument for the existence of God because, as he argues, without the idea of a supreme moral will, moral ideals would not be realizable.

I could in this place enumerate a hundred different, more or less historical, arguments for the existence of God. As noted before, their great number is evidence enough of their lack of convincing power.

## II

The word God has been used to describe supernatural beings. A primitive man before whose eyes a tree is struck by lightning, a cave-dweller watching eruptions of a volcano, a bushman stopping suddenly before a seemingly endless body of water, a group of lake dwellers watching a sick child breathing out its last breath—these must have concluded the existence of supernatural powers, whom the nations of antiquity referred to as gods. To such people, a man piloting a plane or setting off an explosion by pressing a button, or Dillinger firing a sawed-off shotgun would definitely have appeared as divine creatures.

Now, we have learned a good deal in the last 5,000 years, but sometimes it seems that we still work on the same principle of theological reasoning that was used by primitive man. Of course, we know that the ocean isn't endless; we know that the sun is neither driven by a god nor is it god itself. We know that the lava belched by a volcano can be reproduced in the laboratory; we know the causes of rain and lightning and thunder. In fact, we can make these, too, although at present less effectively than nature.

We know that below the crust of the earth flows no Styx but oil—still some of us continue to call on God the minute our off-the-cuff reasoning fails us. To the pagan of old, lightning may have been miraculous—must a sudden spring in Lourdes or elsewhere therefore appear miraculous to us, and must cures effected on pilgrimages to such places be called miraculous? We have seen equally effective cures performed by certain nature quacks and medicine men from here to Timbuktu and Oz. And don't such minds ever wonder why the rest of the sick world of Christians can get no help from the springs, in spite of a million prayers, masses and novenas? But they don't wonder and that is the great tragedy of this hour and all times—the lack of wonderment. Wonderment is the beginning of all true thinking. More, it is true thinking in action.

When the priests of antiquity failed in their oracles and the failure of their prognostications came back to hound them, they always had that one alibi: "It would have worked if you were not such a sinful creature, or maybe someone in your family is a sinner, or maybe you didn't sacrifice enough to the gods."

And so the ancients went out and cheerfully killed their nearest relative to appease a greedy deity. And Agamemnon put his dearly beloved daughter Iphigenia to the torch to go on a military expedition to bring back Menelaus' flirtatious wife from her Trojan jaunt with Paris. Here a man burned his own flesh and blood—a virgin—for a whore who after the death of Paris jumped from one Trojan bed into another. And all that ritual and sacrifice allegedly to appease the lords of Olympus!

Let us not make the same mistake and excuse as some mysterious designs of God the evil and illness and heartbreaking suffering that innocent mankind must endure.

One of the few survivors from the German gaschambers tells the tragic episode of the last conversation he held with the rabbi of his community on the eve of their execution, when the old clergyman still stoutly defended the everlasting wisdom and providence of the Lord Jehovah, in spite of the all too-obvious butcherous extermination by the German people of the Israelites. "If there is purpose in God's seeing and permitting these monstrosities," the young man said to the rabbi, "then God must have in His mind perhaps the increase of Germany's soap and fertilizer output, because that is what they're using our corpses for. There can be no divine providence in tolerating the torturous carnage of all the six million Jews of Europe—men, women, and children. There can be no divine providence so far as the Jews of Europe are concerned, because there are no more Jews left in Europe to benefit by it, or even to take a lesson from it." We do not know what answer the rabbi gave to the laments of the young man who related this episode a few days before his disease-ridden, starved body gave up its spirit in an American military hospital.

The story of this rabbi and the young Jew can be told with a thousand variations, perhaps of less gruesome text, of any thousand years covering any thousand cities. Wars, pestilence, persecutions and nature's bone-breaking games of flood, earthquake and hurricane could tell never-ending tales of human suffering and misery. If anyone tries to see providence or guidance in these accidents and devilish acts, he is fooling himself or convincing the foolish. If the massacre of a million people is considered an act of divine providence, and not a criminal's lustful mania, then perhaps Nero and Hitler and Genghis Khan knew the ways of God better than Isaiah.

If we try to read into accidents and peculiar events secret meanings of divine interference, then we don't reason much more deeply than the bushman under the burning tree, who thinks that God came down from the heavens to put the tree to the torch and teach the bush people a lesson in religion. The person who sees the hand of God in the crippling of a five-year-old boy, or in the unexpected recovery of another child, reasons with rt "THE GOOD GOD AND GOD"

the bushman's mind, and his Christianity is as profound and significant as the faith of the bushman.

To the pagan people of old, the gods were jacks-in-the-box who jumped into their faces whenever the occasion arose. They even jumped into the beds of mortals and fathered or mothered demi-gods and goddesses. Our God is not a jack-in-the-box, and it is sheer blasphemy to make the Lord responsible for the little good and the mountainous mess of evil that dominates this world. In the last ten years alone, 20 million people were put to the sword—and most of them in defense of their lives and the lives of their families. The horrible maiming and bombing of defenseless women and children, these ten years of the mustached werewolf of Berlin, what good can there be in these and to whom? excepting that he and his people had ten glorious years of a hell of a time.

No, we shall not find God in the evil doings of man. And whatever happens in the life of man, the melancholy cask of suffering and the puny thimble of happiness, God has no hand in it, not even a finger—not on your life! We have to search for God elsewhere.

13

### III

If this, our watery globe, which when viewed from a distance of a thousand miles must appear like a piece of Florida swampland, is a divinely devised structure, then what is the nature of this structure—which the Greeks called "physis"? And I do not mean the search for the ultimate units of matter or the study of the particles which make up our global mass and the masses immediately surrounding it.

Our quest is for the mental physics or the scope or meaning of elementary existence. If someone at this point questions our ability to comprehend and our right to analyze the possible purposes of Being, to such a person I would say that we have as little and as much justification in accepting divine structure and purpose as we have in denying it. If we have no right to say "no" to traditional faith and interpretation, then we have no right to say "yes." *Sic* and *non* are just two sides of the same judgment. There is always in back of your "yes" an equally powerful "no." Some merely think they can avoid the issue by turning it about; it is there just the same.

There were men like Gottfried Wilhelm Leibniz, who engaged in a cheerful definition of this world as the best possible of all predestined by God thus to exist. There were men like Arthur Schopenhauer, who thought this the worst possible world. And what kind of world is this anyhow, and what yardstick can we apply to measure good and evil? We choose to call our world the universe. By that we mean our swampy patch of earth and the innumerable rocks and gases that are whirling around us. Perhaps all this gigantic and hectic activity is just whoosh in the wind of the rest of unphenomenal existence of which we are not even aware. Like the tiny worm in man's stomach, you may feel that's all there is to the world—the stomach of man.

But if we speak of God and in our minds and prayers endow him with attributes, our minds must judge whether these attributes are created by the mere traditional monotony of religious repetition or are something more than that. This is especially so since religious traditions vary so much from land to land and people to people. The Italian Catholic genuflecting before an image of Holy Mary will call forth at best a shaking of the head from a Buddhist monk, and the festive Hebrew intoning the blessings of God on Friday night while raising a cup of wine to his lips will at best cause a frown upon the face of a Mohammedan.

Yes, but one might still say, that they all believe in one God! Even if that were true (which it is not—only a minority of the world's population believes in God Creator and God Governor revealing himself or having revealed himself to man)—even if these revelations were true, they could not all be true, and they could not be divine and a blessing to one, and a curse to another.

What is the structure of this our brush and water-covered earth? Upon what principle does this huge swamp and jungle operate? Let us walk down to a brook, any brook. There are countless little insects under the water and above its surface, some feeding on plant life, others on smaller insects. And then there are the fish and the frogs and the birds and the spiders that devour small creatures and big creatures alike. And then there are bigger fish who swallow the small fish and then there are the beautiful flamingo and the romantic stork to eat up the fish and the frog. And then there is the fox who hunts the birds. There is an endless chain of murder in this our swamp and jungle land.

Thus are our living creatures organized—they have to devour each other to live, tear each other apart limb by limb. Whether it is the fighter whale who rips the tongue out of the mouth of the whale cow, or the spider who gnaws at its living victim piece by piece, or for that matter, man who throws a live lobster into the boiler, this wanton and cruel feeding on other creatures is the system upon which life in our world is based. This chain murder is not accidental; it is essential to the existence of these creatures.

If there is purpose or method in this mad process of tearing apart, gulping down and digesting —to call it divine is blasphemy. It is tragic, perhaps, but if it is predestination, then it is a devilish one. If it is premeditation, it is a sinister one. And if it is pre-eminent, as it is, it makes this world a melancholy place. The river you plunge into for a cooling swim is a stinking, foul battleground in which a million creatures are tearing each other to bits every minute of the day. You walk through the meadow in the cool of the evening, and at your feet the insects slash at each other, mad with the greed of their empty insides. Or rest in the forest in the shade of a tree—if you could only hear the dying whimper of the doe slashed by roaming beasts, or the iciest hunter of them all—man. How well Luther said it, "Here in the midst of life we are surrounded by death."

How little did the poets suspect, when they wrote of the inspiring breeze blowing gently through the tree tops, that in this breeze was the stench of a thousand dying creatures, the stench of decaying flesh.

Is there divinity in such purpose?

I do not wish to recount the immeasurable grief, horror and suffering that man has visited upon man since time immemorial: wilful slaughter, burning, torturing. One who has taken even a fleeting glance at man's history knows that it is most painful to contemplate, and it must be said again that the short, the very short, period of our history which we call the Christian era shows not the slightest improvement in this respect over any other period, or what we call the pagan era. In fact, our Christian civilization is, it can be said in all fairness, the most butcherous, the most murderous, the most bloody period known in human history.

Viewing the above I think it is evident that if we point to our messy globe as a harboring place of godly providence and angelic guidance, we are blasphemously sarcastic. This our jungle life, in its ubiquitous predestined mutual destruction, is no haven of divine leadership. We are left here to our own devices of self-protection; and if there is a way by which we can be raised above the level of the rest of the swamp creatures, this way will have to be found by ourselves and be based upon the powers of our own reason and our sense of human justice. Reliance upon allegedly divine purposes has always only served to hoist cowards, tyrants and demagogues upon some theology-supported pedestal from which they drove liberal men to the pyre and the masses to dull subservience. There is nothing divine about this our life and this our globe. But ours can be made a more human habitation if we would stop looking for God behind the clouds, and the devil under the coal mine, and drop bigotry for the sake of humanity.

But if God is not in our life and certainly nowhere in wild nature, where is God?

## IV

It is obvious from the foregoing that it is nigh impossible for any contemporary endowed with a moderate amount of reason to hold belief in an all-merciful, all-knowing and all-present God. It is axiomatically true that it takes the same amount of intelligence and determination, as well as knowledge, to say "yes" to a proposition as it takes to say "no." We have as little authority to assert the existence of a divine power playing interference in world affairs as we have to deny it—this, contrary to some persons' opinions that any fool is perfectly justified in accepting faith and tradition while he who questions or denies or negates faith and tradition is a knave. So rigid have become the chains of servility in man, deliberately forged by the oppressive powers that were and be, that the average man finds it almost natural to bow to the supernatural, horrified at the mere thought of drawing the drapes apart and facing the issues squarely and sincerely. He reminds one of some of the critics of the immortal physicist and astronomer, Galileo Galilei, who were begged to look for themselves through the telescope; but they wouldn't, fearful of what might befall their book-born traditional beliefs.

And what else are the religious beliefs of people all over the world but book-born traditions— by different books at that! What do we know of creation but what a book says? And of the life of Christ? And so few are the books, that distinguished scholars have written volumes denying the very existence of Moses and Christ as well. There are a hundred different religions and a hundred different exegeses of God and gods. To one mortal soul, the son of Mary is God Incarnate; to the other mortal across the river, he is a mere legend around a boy carpenter.

It all depends upon what books you reached first, or rather what books first reached you, for the books we read are not determined by choice but by the accidents of geography and language. Long after the books that make for a certain faith and a certain frame of mind have taken possession of us from the age of 6 to the age of 16, we may be given some choice and we may fit some strange books into this frame of mind. But rarely does one find a man or woman who has the depth and courage and power to splinter that frame and walk out into the open of cosmic thought, a free man or a free woman.

In most instances the overwhelming power of the books has been so effective that we find the most ridiculous statements of our theological literature perfectly reflected in the books of other religions. We can even see the fallacies where they cannot.

Let us put aside the books for a moment and start from the premise: we cannot accept the verity of any traditional proposition unless it conforms to the basic principles of reason and ethics. If we fail to accept this principle, then we are not better than those aborigines of India who, as late as the last century, swore to a belief that encouraged them to massacre human beings to enhance their religiosity and standing before the gods. If reason and ethics are removed from the chair of judgment, then every outrage and animalistic perversion can be made a religious creed. And true enough, this has been done, not only in ancient times, in the sacrifice of humans by the Carthaginians, Greeks, Aztecs and other highly cultured peoples.

We cannot in due respect to our mind and morals accept the existence of God Creator and God Governor interfering in the affairs of man, beast and the world.

So far as beasts are concerned, their lives are tied in such a devilish plan that one must destroy the other in order to exist. Spider must eat insect, fish must eat worm, the big fish devour the small fish, the big bird the small bird, and where there is a lone beast living off the grass, there is always one of the carnivorous creatures ready to pounce upon it and tear it apart. And last but not least, there is man, God's flabby effigy, who smothers, smites and swallows them all, fish, bird and deer. And even the insect is not safe from man's gruesome appetite for flesh and blood. Such is the chain of animal life. It cannot be escaped. It is like the Chinese torture wire trick. If you breathe, it cuts your throat. If you stop breathing, you choke to death. And what a peak of romanticized silliness is the all-helpful God who feeds the birds in the field. Yes—he feeds them— on worms! They feed upon each other, beast after beast after beast in an endless process of prowling, devouring and procreating. What a scheme, what a devilish scheme! It is ridiculous to attribute it to divine planning.

And the world of man—in what does it differ from the world of the beast? It differs in that man participates in two chains of murder. He murders the animals to feed himself, and he murders his neighbors so they may not partake of his venison.

The evidence of human cruelty and bestiality is so overwhelming that to cite instances would beggar its perennial prevalence. Man has cut up man since time immemorial. Man even ate man, although it matters little what happens to the corpses. We hold it less against the Germans that they ground the corpses of the Jews into fertilizer or boiled them into soap or jokingly hung them up in butcher shop windows—we hold it less against them than the fact that they cut them up in the first place. Cannibalism, at least, is butchery with a purpose, while massacre for national or religious reasons is sheer lust murder.

And such has been the life of man that throughout human history wars and executions and bellicose destruction seem to be the rule of human conduct. We have no reason to assume that this conduct was worse in prehistoric times, of which we know nothing, than in the last 2,000 years of the Christian era, of which we know about everything there is to know.

So far as the world itself is concerned, with its earthly calamities of floods, volcanoes and hurricanes which maim, cripple, stone, drown, burn, and bury alive men, women and children by the townful—if anyone attributes that to the wise planning of God, that too is blasphemy. Only Satan could play such havoc with beast, man and earth and then claim mercy and justice as his divine prerogative. Yet we see people aware of this sarcasm genuflect and clasp their hands in prayer to an alleged merciful creator and governor or to his elect and elevated in sainted stone or painting—see them pray for the improvement of their little lives. If they could see, had they the eyes, the unpunished evil being perpetrated by man upon man and by nature upon man—whole countries obliterated, whole nations massacred; tumbling children, tired old people, the weak and the sick bomb-blasted, burned and drowned—and they still keep praying for their race horses to run first, or for Johnny to come home, or for Mary

to get well. *Sancta simplicitas!* As if God had first
to set up a world of murderous people and animals
on a fire-belching and disease-infested earth, so
as to be able to throw little crumbs of favors to a
bunch of prayerful bigots. As if a few favors
dished out to such practiced prayer sharps could
atone for the gigantic and horrible slaughter of
life and this ever-destructive hell on earth. (It is
peculiar to those humans that have the run of our
global sectors that they could find such a sadistic
type of deity as would have to be concluded from
our *Weltbild* were it the subject of divine planning
and creation.) Perfectly acceptable, so long as
they have an opportunity to sneak up to God and
pray for some little concessions for themselves. In
fact, I fear that the great majority is left cold by
the misery of the rest of the world. At any rate, it
seems to trouble little their philosophic and religious views.

I see them devoutly bless the flags of their own
cause, knowing, of course, the right to be on their
side, although the simplest reasoning should indicate to them that if their blessings and prayers
had any value, and if the divine interference for
which they are praying were possible, such inter-

ference could easily have been executed by God Governor without sanguinary battles and the other destruction that wars bring about.

All these prayers, of course, are nothing but expressions of man's selfishly animalistic nature; I have yet to see the day when men will bless the flags of their enemies and pray for the welfare of other nations, not their own.

No, there is little of true divinity in the prayers and hymns of our seemingly religious. The God to whom they are addressing their petitions is nowhere but in their narrow minds and small hearts. And the God who is, they are unaware of.

God is, but God is not on the outside, riding above the clouds with his entourage of Thomistic angels and 50,000 saints. He is not whirling through space with planets and meteors listening to the supplications of selfish bigots prostrate before images and ikons in egotistical obeisance— no, such a God differs little from the Olympic inhabitants of a sophisticated Greece or the divine hierarchies of the ancient Sumerians, Babylonians, Hittites, and Carthaginians.

The ultimate of mental physics, like the ultimate of material physics, is to be found within the being, not outside it. God, or a substance, or the ultimate, is within us, and it is one and it is eternal. *Adonai elohainu, adonai echod*: the Eternal is our God, the Eternal is One. It is the atom of our mind. It is thought creative, thought freed from encumbrances, thought returned to itself, to *ens parennia*, the noumetic idea of Plato, the *tachtuamatsi* of the Indians, the *olam katan* of the Cabala.

That is why the Torah says, "Let no man make a picture of Me." Jahve, there is no God besides Jahve. The name of Jahve shall not be written; it should only be thought. And man is made in the image of Jahve; man is *olam katan*, the little world, the whole world. God is in man; God is man, the innermost of man, the atom of man's ultimate thought, the consciousness of man's unity with the All, which brings with it man's liberation from traditional confusion and prejudice.

From this atom of thought springs not only man's deepest understanding of his time-bound existence on this fleeting planet, but also an unfailing consciousness of all living creatures, for which the word love is only a shallow and much-abused description. There is no God besides the God in the depth of man's mind. There is no love and inner freedom but that springs from the fountain of truly divine cognition. There is no unity but the everlasting truth borne by man's inner self.

All other gods are figments of superstitious thought and deliberate fabrications of the God makers in which the true prophets had no part. The true prophets held the true faith, and when they spoke they were only mouthpieces for the voice of God. God was with them, as I wish He would dwell in the hearts of all the people, so that they might mend their ways and become aware of the inner self, which is the door and the way and the end.

# Prayers That Never Reach
the Heavens

IF PRAYER WERE A FUNCTION TO WHICH THE HUMAN
mind resorts in agony or despair, it would then be
less a theology of communication with the Divine
and stand more accurately as human weakness.
The drowning person grasping for God as for a
halm of straw—is he to be given more credit for
his judgment in terror that either of the two is better than nothing? That goes for the straw halm,
whose buoyancy he must always have deemed
feathery and puny, and the hand of the Lord,
whose very existence he may even have doubted.
The prayers of the mortally terrorized are evidence of no more than stark fear—not fear of sin
or fear of evil or fear of hell and *Gehenna*, but
fear of being choked or smothered or drowned or
cut up.

Still, there are prayers of a Divine nature.

Are they to be found in the pews of those kneeling for better business or heavier wheat or more

plentiful potatoes? Are they to be found among those marching in a procession to conjure a flood of rain from the Heavens or put an end to hail or a plague of locusts? Are they to be found among those prostrated on the deck of a ship, asking for a gentle sea and a bountiful catch of fish? Are they to be found among the priests and preachers blessing the flags and weapons of their own armor in the coming combat against similarly blessed instruments of war?

Are they to be found in the sickroom, where a mother begs for the health and life of her child? Are they to be found on the trapeze where the gymnasts make the sign of a cross before the *salto mortale*? Are they to be found at the hazard table in the gambling room, where the gods are called upon to fix a number for the chap with his last quid? Certainly, if those are prayers they never go beyond the earshot of man and wherever the winds and waters may carry them, they never, never reach the ear of the Lord.

The Lord doesn't make little children sick so that prayers, no matter how ardent and anxious, may make Him heal one and let a thousand others perish or remain alive, crippled and blinded and sore—as they do. It would be a terrible God who made these few exceptions among the victims of the hydra of accident and sudden death. God has no hand in the horrible self-perpetuating machine of our globe. How little do they think of Him who believe that He lets so many beings become maimed, broken and gangrened just to get a few paternosters and perhaps spares those most dextrous with the rosary beads.

Do those who bless the cannon feel that the angels of the Almighty guide the balls to make certain of their aim and assure destruction among the soldiers of the enemy, who probably have offered equivalent prayers? What blasphemy to tie the pennant of the Lord to the bloody bayonets. It is not in God they believe but in Lucifer, and it is Lucifer's work they do.

There is only one pennant belonging to the Lord, and that is peace of mind. *Shalom* is the pennant of God, and *shalom* means peace. And he who prays for anything but peace is not communicating with God but is just a frail being in despair, or a person eager for position, or a schemer out for no good who uses the most saintly name as a cloak to hide his devious designs. The ancient Hebrews did not dare or permit such usage of the name of the Lord. And how vainly has our civilization called upon this name of names. The prophets of Israel and the rabbis of old bitterly denounced lip prayers and called for *Kavvanah,* for the yearning of the heart.

Where the heart does not long for love eternal and peace among men there is no communication with the Divine; there is no true prayer. Prayer is the pining of the soul of man for the soul eternal, in this aimlessly drifting world of evil and illness, pain and deceit. It is prayer alone that raises man's heart to the Heavens. Blessed are those who feel that yearning of the heart go deeper and deeper.

# Christ Stopped at Georgia

WERE IT NOT FOR A FEW FORTUNATE MILITARY successes of the Northern armies under President Abraham Lincoln, we might still, in this twentieth century, have slavery in our country. We are inclined to think of the past, even the recent past, as a primitive period, frequently unmindful of the fact that we differ only in fashion and degree from the primitivity of the past. Our grandfathers and their parents who kept slaves, bonded Christian humans, trading them on the open market like cattle, in fact, frequently exchanging one for the other, considered themselves as living on a high plateau of religious and cultural accomplishment.

At this writing, there is a group of countries, including Yemen, Saudi Arabia, and Abyssinia, that either deals in slaves, or keeps them. For sundry slimy and oily reasons the Western World has done little to wipe out this barbaric practice but instead prefers to continue its deals with perfumed and bearded crooked heads, ignoring the sorrowful and villainous institutions upheld by the dastardly rulers.

How much better are we than our grandfathers were? They gave good and economic reasons, even quoting Scripture, to support their enslavement of the black man—and the descendants of those slaveholders give good and economic reasons for forcing the black man to walk in the gutter or take a rear seat. As for quoting Scripture in justification of Christian rancor, I have heard tell that Lucifer can quote Scripture as well, or nearly as well, as the white preachers from Georgia or Alabama.

Why is it that man permits such indignities to be done to man? How come that your dear grandpappy could stand before a platform upon which were lined up a group of Christians who differed from him and his flock only by the slightly darker tint of their skin and the kink in their hair—and your smiling sweet grandpappy would watch the men being felt like horses, thighs, biceps and teeth examined, and thrown to the highest bidder; and Christian girls were inspected for the quality of their breasts and other sexual characteristics, under the sneers and snickers of a tobacco-chewing gentry.

How come your sweet smiling grandpappy could stomach this and find nothing wrong in it, shrewdly participating in this trade of human flesh.

Your grandpappy is dead now, but there are others down south and up north who see enough of the black man's misery and humiliation to make their hearts cry out in compassion—were there a conscience in their hearts.

Compassion is the voice of conscience; where there is no conscience, no compassion will ever rise.

They walk into eating places where no black man will be served; they enter homes where no black man is ever permitted, unless in servitude; they march into their high and mighty offices where no black man may work, except in servitude. And lend an ear, my good Lord: They congregate in church to venerate Your humility, Your all-embracing love, but no "nigger" may pass through the portals of Your cross-adorned edifice —there is a little door in the back, marked in paint and neglected: "For Colored Only." I wonder if Your gate-keeper, Peter, my dear Lord, has such a shabby backdoor?

As for quoting the Bible, let us take, for instance, the issue of escaped slaves. In Deuteronomy it is clearly stated: "Thou shalt not deliver unto his master the servant who has escaped from his master unto thee. He shall dwell with thee, even among you in that place which he shall choose in one of thy gates where it liketh him best. Thou shalt not oppress him." So does the Torah deal with an escaped slave. The New Testament, on the other hand, is full of lofty sentiments and generalities which can be interpreted this way and that way. The Torah is a book of law, and as such is concrete and definite. Who has not heard of the answer a Southern Christian preacher gave to a rabbi who in the heydays of slave-holding reprimanded him for encouraging a posse to hunt for an escaped Negro slave. "Why, don't you know, heathen," said the preacher to the rabbi, "it says in the gospels 'Give to Caesar what is Caesar's'." Thereupon the rabbi, astounded, queried, "But how about the love for thy neighbor?" And the preacher replied, "We sure love them, them poor creatures, but we love them the way God made them, black, ugly, dumb and loyal. Them that run away are just not loyal; they are just bad niggers and bad Christians." So you see how one can twist the New Testament. It took an awful lot of twisting in the whole two-thousand-year era of Christian dominance to justify slavery and serfdom all over Europe, Asia and America.

At no time were slaves treated with greater cruelty, greater disregard for human rights, than in the Christian era of Western civilization. The ancient peoples of Asia, Africa and the Mediterranean frequently selected enslavement as a lesser punishment for conquered nations, instead of extermination. Among the Greeks and Romans one found slaves receiving considerable consideration, given positions in the field of learning, in the field of art, and the opportunity of emancipation under certain conditions. The only people who made abolition of slavery compulsory after a length of time were the ancient Hebrews. Here again we find the Hebrews carrying the torch of higher civilization, before all the other nations and races of the globe. The Hebrew was compelled to set his slave free after a number of years, and he was admonished not to let him go empty-handed, but to give from his stock and his capital, so that the former slave might not be in want.

Only in the Christian era do we find the serf chained to his ground by the unmitigated callousness, selfishness and greed of the authorities. The serfs of Europe had as little chance to rise above their miserable position as the black man of America in the eighteenth and nineteenth centuries.

Some Christian historians and philosophers attempt to attribute the rising freedom of the last one hundred and fifty years to an awakening and spreading of Christian culture. The contrary is the truth. So long as Christian culture prevailed, the masses of Europe, the blacks of America, the Jews wherever they were, lived in castigated bondage. It took revolutions and wars in America and France to break the absolutistic dominance of authoritarian powers. Freedom, however little or much of it we have today, came not through or because of Christianity, but in spite of it.

These are the facts; let us face them. Freedom did not come to us reflected in the benign countenances of a self-satisfied clergy, but in the blood and anguish of rebels, through the sufferings of men like Thomas Paine, Benjamin Rush,

John Brown, and Abraham Lincoln. And those who brought freedom to Europe with the beginning of the peasant revolts during the Reformation, they did not carry the cross, they carried the pitchfork.

The cross was with the aristocrats; it was and sometimes still is with those who run plantations and trade in land and live off vested interests.

Certainly there were men of conscience in the Western hemisphere, men and women who recognized the issues at stake and to whom the true motives of slaveholding were not obscure. From the Greek Hippias to Abraham Lincoln, there were men and women of conscience and nobility who threw the lie in the face of common perfidy and hypocrisy. But courage implanted with wisdom is a rare flower indeed, and weeds are plentiful. Why the good Lord has endowed so few with conscience and compassion is something I cannot fathom.

The many many are deaf to the cries of sufferers outside their clan—and don't they tolerate abominations against those whom they stamp down and hold inferior? It flatters their little souls to be considered better than a whole race of people, be it the Jewish race or the African race or the Chinese. The emptier the person so much more swiftly will slogans of alleged superiority blow him up and inflate him so that he appears—at least to himself—as something better, or at least as a higher being.

Because of his assumed superiority above others, the man of nothing becomes a being. It is so easy and pleasant and flattering to mingle with the dominant; and arduous, on the other hand, to join the down-trodden whose path becomes dangerous when they are marching up.

But up they will go and up they will come, and the palaces and the temples of the vicious oppressors will fall in the dust.

Truth moves slowly, but its path is unbending, and its goal is sure and its goal is tomorrow—and can't you smell the sweetness of the dawn?

# God at the Crossroads

THE GOOD LORD IS AT THE CROSSROADS. SOMETHING epochal will have to occur to reinstate Him in the heart of man, or He will vanish into oblivion, like Jupiter, Armuzd, and Wotan. It seems almost as if time were running out on the Christian God. Or is it that the devil has won in the struggle for supremacy over man's heart?

A casual glance at the news should give even the most optimistic observers the intelligence that there is blackness in the heart of Western man and bleakness in the heavens. The record of the defenders of the Christian Lord is spattered with the blood of pagans, and Christians as well; if the Lord sent His own Son to bring peace to this earth, it seems the Prince of War was always one step behind the Prince of Peace. Why is Christianity such a dismal failure? There can be nothing wrong with those ancient Hebrew teachings of "Love your neighbor," or "Do not to your neighbor what you don't want done to yourself," or

perhaps even "Love your enemy," although all
these sayings, which had their origin among the
fishermen and shepherds of the Jordan valley,
sound rather ludicrous when mouthed by monks
accompanying armies of conquistadores or missionaries financed by oil companies or the admirals
of European fleets attempting to expand some
imperialist's power.

You can't find room for the good Lord in the
hearts of men when conversion is made with a
bloody sword.

When Cortez choked the trusting Montezuma,
when the Pizarro brothers garroted Atahualpa,
when the British slave hunters roamed the plains
of Africa, driving human game—did they and
others of their profession really imagine they could
ram Christianity down the minds of their victims?
And in later years, when the hold of the West
became more firmly established but less cruel,
although the people of the West continued to re-
gard the men and women of Asia and Africa as
third rate creatures, good enough to exploit but
not good enough to sit with at table, did Westerners really think that by contempt and maltreat-
ment, by avarice and selfishness, by greed and

belligerence they could induce the people of Asia and Africa to sacrifice their customs and beliefs for the sake of the Christian religion which the Westerners wore as a mask to cover their ugly faces?

Western man has hatched in Asia a devil's egg, and it now has come home to roost.

Will the white man ever learn that cars and radios and frigidaires do not make a civilization? And so far as the Asiatics and Africans are concerned, these people still have few of these gadgets of exterior culture. What they wish for much more earnestly than possession of these contrivances is a feeling of equality with the white man; an equality promised hollowly by the Christians and then denied in practice.

To the Asiatic, Christianity, and especially the Christians, appears as a grand joke, a grim joke, one not at all funny. In India, in North Africa, in the Malayas, in China, for hundreds of years the men preaching the sermons of Christ and the Commandments of the Lord were breaking the latter and contradicting the former with every act. A few hundred thousand Christian strangers took it upon themselves to appropriate all civil, judicial, and military rights from millions of people. In their own country the natives could not ride in the same train with the strange invaders; they were not permitted in the same eating places with the strange invaders; they were not admitted to the performances, schools, games and theatres of the strange invaders. The inhabitant of India or Tunisia or the Malayas had no voice in electing his own government and its officials. Yet with full knowledge of this fact he was expected to accept such a regime as based upon the highest principles of modern civilization and the divine rights of the Christian nations.

Europe, Asia and Africa were conquered by the sword. The Cross always came as an afterthought, and while the Asiatics and Africans could quickly grasp the power of the European sword, they somehow never got the afterthought into their heads. The good Lord was smuggled in to them in a Trojan horse.

The conquerors spoke of Christ but they meant gold; they spoke of Christ but they meant rubber; they spoke of Christ but they meant pearls. The good Lord is in a bad way in Asia and Africa and perhaps all over this little globe. His spokesmen are double tongued. Too many times have His churches sided with the oppressor, and so rarely with the people.

Perhaps if the Lord were to drop His churches the people would take heart. Perhaps the churches are the Lord's unwelcome protagonists, self-appointed friends who drag His name down with their evil deeds. The people of Asia and Africa, as well as the rest of the world, have been preyed upon by vicious and selfish imperialists with priests and monks, preachers and missionaries following at their heels.

The good Lord is about to lose this globe. There is little room left for honest faith in the sight of all the evil that predominates from century to century; wars and pestilence, enslavement and oppression, exploitation and wars again. I don't think the good Lord lives any longer in the hearts of men, only in churches and cemeteries.

The people don't act as though they ever put much stock in the Commandments of the Lord and the love sermons of Christ, and it isn't much of a God who inhabits church spires and mausoleums.

God must be alive, a burning flame in the soul of man, so that man may become kind and helpful and generous to his fellow man. God is at the crossroads. Unless He does something epochal to the life of His professors, He will drop into oblivion like Jupiter, Armuzd, and Wotan.

# Forgotten Religions

IT MAY BE OF SIGNIFICANCE THAT WILLIAM PENN, the most devout of men, who said "Religion is nothing else but love of God and Man," and Thomas Paine, the most irreverent, who said "All mankind are my brethren, and to do good is my religion," came so close in their definitions of theistic concept.

Western believers have been laboring under the illusion that religion (a word derived from the Latin *religio*—binding) began some time within the last few thousand years; in fact, they even speak of the "origin of religion." They place it within as shallow a time scheme as their archaeology reveals. But undoubtedly men were bound to each other before they became bound to the gods, and religion gripped their hearts before they grasped images of the Divine.

From time immemorial, the oceans of history have been seething, and how tiny and tepid is the pond of the recent past that we can see. Although the men of ages past didn't write to leave us a record of their activities, although they didn't build pillared palaces and paved roads, they still loved, and were more closely bound to God and mankind, perhaps, than we have ever been in our modern epochs of organized religions, which may have ennobled our slogans, but didn't stop our slaughters.

Organized religions have frequently stood with their backs to the past like the eagle on the ledge, as if the mountain were nonexistent except for that little rock. They even began to record time as of their beginning. "They brought the light"; before them, therefore, must have been *Tohu Vavohu*. At this writing there are more than one hundred different "beginnings of time," of which the better known are those of the Christians, Hebrews, Mohammedans, Shintos, Confucians, Buddhists.

There they are, holding on to the coat-tails of aeonic Father Time like a squirrel on the branch of a towering redwood tree, whispering "This is mine."

Eternal Man does not belong to these modern religious groups that battle with each other like

brutes in the jungle. This swarm of ritualism belongs in a little nook in the hallways of Father
Time. There is more to the world than the niche
we know. Let us turn round and take a fleeting
glance at Man's infinite past, which we may never
know, but which we can ponder.

Perhaps a hundred thousand years ago, on the
very ground upon which you are reading these
lines, men were living together—men, women and
children, friends and companions—bound by feelings for each other and considerations for the
young and the old. If such feelings had not
chained their souls to each other, they could not
have survived the hardships and dangers of beast-
infested lands and learned to make tools for use
and comfort and formed hamlets, villages and
communities. There could have been no communities without communion.

What drew the men of these early days to each
other? What made them join together to fight
the animals and other common enemies and
hardships? Was that not religion?

If friendship to man and a love for justice and
peaceful communal life are not religion, what are
they? And what is religion without friendship and

love for justice and for a peaceful communal life? True enough, traditions and ritual heritage accompany religion, but they are only the wreaths and flowers that decorate the chain. For if that inner binding of justice and kindness to all men does not exist inherently, religions could not hold together by themselves. They would fall apart like the flimsies they are.

Some persons believe that religion is a binding to God, that man can tie himself to the Lord with rituals and obeisances. Not a thousand rosaries could entwine the hardened soul to the heavens, and all the genuflecting of the bigot will not brighten the darkness of a callous mind before the Lord. Only the Divine in mind can find this symphonic resonance in the celestial spheres; for love to man and love to God and love of God to man are but three links of the one chain. The Hebrew Spinoza named it *amor dei intellectualis* —the spiritual love of God.

# The Devil Who Came to Stay

THE WORST THING ABOUT THE DEVIL IS THAT MOST people flatly deny his existence. Obviously he can thus do considerable damage to body and soul without ever being blamed. The devil is like Siegfried, storming over the planet with the *Tarnkappe* across his horns, seen by no one but seeing all; at least all the devil cares to see.

I don't rightly know why the devil prefers to use the tricky device of Hitler's Teutonic Nibelungen hero, but that is neither here nor there.

The devil has been with us for a long, long time—much longer than the good Lord, who stayed away from paleolithic man of the cave days for a million years.

The Book tells us that it is fewer than six thousand years since the good Lord bent His ears and listened to what we proudly call the crown of His creation, and it is less than half of this time since He sent His Own Son to visit animal-man. And what a reception they gave Him!

And this in spite of the Lord's coming being well announced by the prophets, kings, and judges who gave animal-man the ten commandments, books of law, and wise admonitions. But somehow it seems that with the word of God inscribed on scrolls in big Hebrew letters by the prophets themselves and the kings and the judges, there is more unholiness and ungodliness now than there ever was before Moses spotted the back of Jehovah on Mount Sinai. Perhaps the Master came too late, because during all the million years of Jehovah's absence the devil was squatting right next to man. He slept in his cave; he sat at his campfire. He helped him poison his arrows. The devil has ungodly cunning—and the devil is no gentleman.

I do not know, and I doubt whether anyone else knows, why the devil chose man as his bosom companion and why not the tiger, the condor, or even the deer. They should make better vessels for carrying evil. For there is no good in the condor, or tiger, or shark. They just live to eat and forni-cate. They never, never have any desire to be helpful or to do good. But there is no devil in the tiger, the shark, or the condor. If they eat grass, or carcass, they eat to still their appetite and then wander off. There is no devil in them. They have no circuses like the Romans who made a sport of throwing unarmed and helpless slaves to fierce, starved beasts. There is no devil in these animals. Have you ever heard of a tiger who would chain another tiger to a tree and make him his slave for the rest of his life? There is no devil in these animals. They do not act like the humans who roamed the plains of Africa and dragged to a foreign soil a million black men chained and starved, forever to be their servants. They do not go out armed with axes and spears and guns bent on expeditions of conquest, cutting the bodies of other beings; thus with their victims' blood and breath freedom flows away—and this has been done from the days of Rameses to Nero, from Genghis Khan to Cortez, from Attila to Hitler.

The shark and the tiger and the condor, they simply eat their fill and wander away. They know not the human hunger for tyranny, conquest and oppression, or the ways of torture which man has invented and practiced—the rack, the iron Jungfrau, burning alive, skinning alive. There is no devil in these animals.

But man is a cultured being. He shoves Jewish children into a stove today and tomorrow he goes to Salzburg to listen to a Mozart concert. He vivisects a Jewish woman today and tomorrow he kneels before the Passion Play of Oberammergau.

Once the devil was almost killed. Luther threw a bottle of ink at him. You can still see the blot on the wall. But Luther obviously missed because the devil never really left the borders of Germany.

In the olden days, men thought you had to make a regular contract with the devil, as Faust did, with blood instead of ink, following a definite ritual. But that isn't really so. The devil is always there. He is ubiquitous, like the microbes; it is just that you have to have resistance. And that is what makes it so difficult, for it was only in later years that the Lord revealed Himself. And Lucifer has been with us for a million years. He is the small voice that always pipes up at the wrong moment with that all powerful squeak, "What for?" "Why should I?" "Why not?" "Kill that so and so."

You all know the voice of the devil. And if you don't by now, you never will. Did you ever watch a mob at a lynching? Or even at a good beating? Look at their faces and you can see the devil.

Once I even saw him in church in Germany. The Vicar announced from the pulpit that the burning of Jews was all right because the Lord said we should love our neighbors and we should love our enemies. But the Jews, the Vicar said, claimed they were not the enemies of Germany and they certainly were not its neighbors.

That just shows how clever is the devil. And clever he is indeed, and quite educated. In fact, in universities he is considerably in the vogue. You know, of course, that some of these institutions of higher learning frown upon giving a classroom seat to a Negro or a Jew, which is a good piece of deviltry in itself. And in Germany, which I might call the home of Beelzebub, the devil must have been a member of the medical association, because that association organized some unspeakable experiments performed on living Jews and Jewesses, the horror of which I will spare you. By all that, we must assume that the devil is something of a college man.

There is, of course, a way of trapping the devil in little things. When you hear that in your town there is to be a lynching, the devil will tell you, "Go out to watch and give a hand! It's only a

nigger! He is not like I am. That can never hap-
pen to me. I am white!"

If the devil thinks you are a softy, he will never
talk like that to you. That would only offend you.
He will tell you, "Oh, what can I do? It's no skin
off my neck. I'm not doing it. Oh, well, there
always will be lynchings and always will be kill-
ings. I can't change the whole world." And you
just stay home and keep reading the funnies or
watch television.

So, you see, in any way that the devil talks, he
has got you, and you can't hear the other voice,
the far-away voice of the Lord: "He who fails to
take up the cause for the oppressed is not less
guilty than the oppressor; for the sin of omis-
sion is as great as the sin of commission." But the
voice of the devil is steady and loud. The voice of
the Lord is a mere whisper. Sometimes I think it
is like that shrill call which only the animals can
hear.

# The Devil in the Tongue

LEGEND HAS IT THAT THERE WAS ONCE A KING IN Egypt who sent for his priest and asked him to cut out for him the best and the worst part of a sacrificial animal. And the priest sent him the animal's tongue with a note reading, "The tongue is the best part for it carries the soothing words of friendship and the whisper of love, and it is the worst part for it is the bearer of the sting of hate and humiliation."

Tongues have made history, from the days of the flaying tongues of the prophets to the tongue twisters of our day. What a different world this might be if men were to be judged by what they do instead of by what they say. It is the tongue that sets man against man, group against group and race against race. There is the tale of the Greek philosopher who when he went to sleep always kept his mouth covered with his right hand so that his tongue might do no mischief while unguarded.

# THE DEVIL IN THE TONGUE

How few can really say, "I am the guardian of my tongue." You can stroll down the street and up the street and you will see a hundred people working their tongues, saying unkind things about strangers and even their own neighbors of this different color, or that different faith, or those different habits. They deal out rips of the tongue which cut into the very heart of the victim.

Perhaps some of the evil words spoken leave a sweet taste in the mouth of the speaker. For why else would he say them? It must be the sweetness of corruption.

Every fifth American spits out the word "Nigger" with a sordid glee. Perhaps it makes him feel big and strong and white. But hurling this word of invective is a distasteful way for a little yellow man to elevate himself above the black man.

The tongue is the heart's mirror.

There must be some good in man or there could not be so much evil. Conversely, if there were no good at all there could be no faith and trust and comradeship, but only savagery and fear as in the days of the cave men. And man would not live with man; he would live alone in a hole in a rock like a reptile.

There is evil because there is good in man. Man is a social being, as the Greek philosopher said, and because of that he is trusting and believing.

But the instinct of the cave man has not died out. The instinct of man to club a fellow man and then spring back to his own shelter remains. Only today the club is replaced by a vicious tongue and the shelter is the spider web of Western Christian civilization that sees no evil, hears no evil, and smells no evil. Of course, in this web we will find men who head cathedrals and colleges and auditoria wherein they speak a great deal of the good but scarcely ever speak of evil. To every fifth man in their cathedrals, their colleges, and their auditoria, the black man is still a "Nigger" but they would rather not talk about that.

I venture to say that the men and women who run our churches and schools could destroy the Hydra of race hatred in one year were they to stand up and speak earnestly of the great evil.

Sermons about the angels and the good life will not drive the devil away. You've got to get him by the tail and call out in a loud and clear voice, "Did any of you in my audience ever say Nigger? Or Kike? Or Chink?

"Did any one in my audience ever permit a black man to be turned away from a desired vacant seat in a theater or church or eating place?

"Did any one in my audience ever refuse a black man a vacant flat in his house or a vacant office in his building?

"Did any one in my audience ever refuse a black boy or girl any desired vacant seat in his school, library, or college?

"Did any one ever refuse a black person a job amongst white employees?

"If so, let him stand up and repent or be cast out from a society which bases its principles upon the teachings of Christ, who came from the people whose greatest prophet was Moses, a son of the Nile—a 'Nigger.' "

# Amor Apostolorum

THE WORD "LOVE" BELONGS IN THAT SMALL GROUP
of general terms that is used more frequently to
disguise an intent or a thought than to divulge
it. And if "love" is used in combination with
"humanity," the word becomes the most dangerous befogger of them all. Members of the English
Church burned their Quaker neighbors out of an
uncontrollable love for dissident humanity. And
the Germans of recent persuasion eliminated eight
million Slavs and Jews out of a love for purified
Aryan humanity.

Love is a dangerous word because it wears the
cloak of unselfishness and has the bearing of traditional dignity. The parent who brutally castigates
his children, acting under a Neronic impulse in
order to satisfy a flabby ego, all the while protests
that his actions are caused by love for his offspring; the power-greedy politician who rides the
broomstick of personal ambition rough-shod over
the welfare of his country, at the same time de-

claims and declares his unending love for God and Fatherland; that wide-grinning, back-slapping pal who with others of his ilk always clusters around the green that can be put in the wallet, that pal who talks sweetly and will always lend you his loving ear in subtle exchange for more tangible leases on your part, that pal of whose kind the wealthy have so many and the impoverished so few—that pal just loves you.

And yet Disraeli said, "Love is the principle of existence and its only end."

Love *is* the principle of existence. Love of oneself is. The body of man in the uncanny wisdom of its natural state exists by the principle of love. The lid will drop to protect the eye; the arm will stretch to prevent a fall; the hand will rise to protect the face—the eternal principle of love makes the very existence of natural man possible. This love instinct is man's dominant factor.

Man can love only himself and the brood which is part of himself. Every other kind of alleged love is just so much talk: talk out of a confusion of facts and concepts, or talk in a deliberate camouflage of motives that cannot risk being bared.

Man can love only himself, and man's body, in

its bodily wisdom, knows which of its parts are the most precious. Instinctively man will parry a blow with his arm or leg. He will never put his head out to stop a knife aimed against his arm. Man loves himself; he must love himself to exist.

In matters outside the body, however, man is oftentimes a poor judge of which things are the most precious. Overbearing tradition, perpetuated by muddled and on occasion evil-purposed followers, has done much to confound and corrupt man's naive heart, and frequently, indeed, such corruption has travelled under the banner of love. They set man against man and child against parent in the devious doctrines of their love propaganda. They befuddle their minds; they befog all the true issues; they get them tongue-tied and out, blaring like cattle with their "Love your neighbor," "Love for God," "Love for the masses," "Love for Christ," "Love for Mohammed," "Love for the caste," "Love for white supremacy," "Love for the Fatherland," "Love for the proletariat," "Love for the elite," "Love for the king"—love for everything excepting the only thing a man can truly love, namely, himself. I shall not burden the patience of the reader with tales of the cruelties that were perpetrated by these love preachers and love tyrants in the name of one kind of love or another. Under the guise of love, man's bestiality to man is matched only by his indifference to the sufferings of others.

If only man would stop loving humanity and deity and begin to love just himself—not that in himself which is on the lowest rung of man, but rather that in himself which occupies the highest rung.

The Talmud says, "Everything begins in the mind—sin and virtue, charity and evil-doing, godliness and deviltry." Love, too, begins in the mind, but the mind does not work by instinct as does the body. The mind does not instinctively raise an arm to protect the eyes. Many are the times when the mind sticks out its head to protect something that is most worthless.

The mind of man must grow by reason to answer the true values in man's inner life. Man can and will always love only himself, but instead of placing his best and his brood and his fellows into servitude before the wintery gods of theoretical love, machinated by conniving tyrants and their priests, he may turn from heathendom, serving before the altar of his own inner self.

Whoever becomes aware of the oracular words "Know thyself" stands in awareness of man's being a link in the chain of universal oneness. Man's soul is just one of the eternal Ideas of this noumetic cosmos. As the ancient Hindus called to man, "Whatever you see is you—the world in you." Love yourself and you love every creature and you love creation. *Natura naturans*, God Creator.

Such love is true love—"*Sub specie aeternitatis*" as Spinoza named it—and in this deepest sense, the love of man to God and the love of man to man are one and the same thing.

There is no true love but the love of man to himself. There is, though, this difference: Is it the love of a greedy mind for things that the ugliest spirits in man conjure, or is it the kind of love that comes from the depth of the soul where heart and intellect meet the essence of creative being?

The man who loves his inner self will find it in all creatures, in all beings, and of his charity and understanding there is no end. In the Torah, the word for *knowing* and the word for *love* are one and the same. He who knows the substance of our life as we whirl through the universe on this piece of rocky crust must feel in the depths of his cognition the unity of the one and all, and the love for his inner self is but the love for the Idea of the Eternal. Only the self-loving man is a God-loving man; the un-selfish man who has not discovered his own self is at best a God-fearing man, and we have seen what havoc those un-selfish men have brought upon mankind in their fear of God.

Turn about and look back at the past 2,000 years and see what these un-selfish men in their fear of God, in their God-commanded love of neighboring humanity, have committed in torture, *auto-da-fé* and plain bloody conquest. Every Christian church in the Western world could be filled to the belfry with the corpses of the men, women and children massacred in the name of love for Christ and in the name of the love-teachings of Christ. That God-intoxicated Hebrew upon whose ardent Mosaic sermons churches were built with so much pretense and so little charity—if that immortal Jew could only see the million agonized faces of the men and women put to the rack and the torch, the rope and the sword, by those who call themselves after Him, the *Christ*; if Christ had come to earth in our time, He would have had to see His mother perish in a German stove, and not a single cry would He have heard from five hundred million Christians. She would have burned to ashes along with the other six million of Christ's brothers and sisters in blood.

"Love thy neighbor" is the teaching that has failed utterly because man can love only himself, his inner self or his ugly self, the inner man or the outer man; but he can never love the other man. Man can love the other man or God Himself only through his inner self, his awareness of being one with all and one in all.

The whole disastrous collapse of Christian civilization, which should be obvious to the most superficial observer of history, is based upon the love pretense of a religion that tears man from his own Self in an attempt to bind him in obedience and adoration to an academic love principle anchored on God, whom you can know and love only through your inner soul; anchored on Christ, a devout Hebrew whose self-awareness the followers of their religion never comprehended; anchored on the Holy Ghost, against whom they have sinned in their secular unholy conquests and cruelties towards the down-trodden—a sin which can never be forgiven.

They preach the love of God and then go out and kill the people from among whom God chose His only Son. They preach "Love thy neighbor" and go out and keep the black man in bondage, terror and humiliation. They preach "Love humanity" and then go out and bless the weapons of war.

Their love is not a love indeed; it is a cloak for their heartless and Godless doings. Perhaps some day man will see through the sham of the pretentious and find a way to his inner self and the love of it which makes man free and understanding and carries charity in its path.

# Jew-baiting and the Holy Ghost

ANTI-SEMITISM IS A LATINIZED TERM DESCRIBING systematic Jew-baiting. It was coined by the German Wilhelm Marr about 1879. It is the only word in any modern language denoting antagonism towards a particular people. There is, for instance, no such word as "anti-Chinism," or "anti-Indianism," or "anti-Swedism," but the Western World needed some learned-sounding term of opprobrium to cover up its robust traditional Jew hatred. The Germans especially were delighted with this coinage. The word carried so much fascination for them that many of their leaders proudly called themselves anti-Semites, although the Jews played little or no role in their lives. Scholastic organizations, professional societies and student fraternities proudly added the word "anti-Semitic" to their lengthy titles as if it were an adjective of some academic distinction.

Why the Germans took to that new word with such fervor is difficult to explain, except perhaps through Adlerian psychology. For centuries the Germans, especially the Prussians, had been striving for a place in the European sun, for a good place, such as the French and British had. This up-hill struggle developed in the Teutons the typical inferiority feeling of the upstart, for which they tried to compensate by a brutal show of force (their continuous wars of aggression since Frederick the Great); an immense display of uniforms (every German had some type of uniform in his closet—some as many as six different ones); and last, but not least, by the ruthless suppression of weaker minorities (small groups of Jewish citizens who constituted less than one percent of the population of Bismarck's Reich).

It is not surprising, therefore, that with the philosophy of anti-Semitism Chamberlain, Gobineau and Richard Wagner found among the Germans an enthusiastic following whence grew the literature of over one hundred thousand books and pamphlets—one hundred thousand publications devoted to nothing but the concept that Jew hatred is a good thing to foster, the various good reasons for this good thing, and why such a good thing in its goodness is good for the rest of mankind, in this case, the Western world of Christian civilization.

Now Jew hatred, like all hatreds of people or nations, is an evil and an unChristian thing, although no one but a Christian ever entertained it seriously. Mohammed had some grievances against the Jews and was occasionally peeved, as were the Caliphs later when the Jews preferred to remain infidels before Allah, but Mohammed was proud of his Abrahamic ancestry and respectfully referred to the Jews as "The People of the Book." By and large, the Mohammedans gave the Jews fair treatment; in fact, during the holocaust of the Iberian inquisitions and the Russo-Polish massacres, the Mohammedan lands were the only permanently safe refuge open to the Hebrews.

Hatred of the Hebrews existed when the Hyksos entered Egypt only to be enslaved and kept in bondage until their victorious revolt and exodus under Moses; Jew hatred existed when the Jews fought their war against the Moabites, the Philistines, the Assyrians and other neighboring nations; Jew hatred existed when the Jews refused to knuckle under the Roman yoke; and Jew hatred has persisted century after century after century.

But those hatreds were the national and temporary animosities of warring nations. They were nothing like the hatred that the Western Christian world tolerated—even nursed—almost as a logical supplement to Christian love. To our shame it must be said that the children of our Western hemisphere have been raised on two breasts—love for man, and hate for the Jew. So deepset became Jew hatred in our civilization that the massacre of tens of thousands of Polish Jews by the Cossack Hetman Chmelnizki in the seventeenth century, or the expulsion, torture and burning of eight hundred thousand Jews in Spain and Portugal in the fifteenth century, or the blood baths among the Jews of the Rhine enacted by the butchering German crusaders in the eleventh century didn't even cause a ripple in the conscience of Christendom. Why the Teutons and the Gallics, the Iberians and the Saxons, the Gauls and the Slavs deemed it unnecessary to apply the principle of Christian love to the Hebrews cannot be understood. Didn't the Lord choose His son from amongst the outcasts of Canaan? Didn't He bless the Jewish Miriam as mother of the Incarnate? Didn't Christ choose His apostles from among the people of

Israel, and not Mesopotamia and not Rome and not Egypt? Didn't the words of Jesus come from the lips of Paul, who in his younger days was Saul, the Talmudic student?

Why, then, do so many think they can still remain Christians if they offer love to their neighbor, but venom to the Jew? If Christ came to earth today, He would feel strange in the huge cathedrals, club rooms and church bazaars. He would be in anguish at what the churches of Germany have tolerated—even endorsed—in fiendish and torturous murder of His brethren. He would be horrified at how a segment of the world that names itself for His calling could hear the children of Israel cry in anguish and terror before the Teutonic onslaught and not raise a hand to stay the bludgeoning arm.

If Christ came to earth today, He, too, would fail to comprehend why His teachings were applicable only to people without the Jordan Valley. Perhaps He would ask of us, "Aren't My brethren people too? Would you smite My brothers and sisters and their offspring? Would you smite offspring of those who carry My gospel? Aren't they as worthy as the Iberians or the Teutons? The first to hear My gospel were the sons and daughters of Israel. It was they—as few as they were—but it was they who gave this world My teachings and the Church!"

While Hebrew shepherds and fishermen listened to the sermons, the people of Europe were kneeling before pagan altars. To many of those nations who carry the devil of Jew hatred in their hearts, the glory of Christ could be made clear only by the thrust of the sword.

If He came to earth today, He would never forgive us, in all His celestial beatitude, for the unspeakable atrocities perpetrated on His kin and the kin of His mother and His faithful believers. All the paternosters and all the hymns of all fifty thousand saints and all fifty thousand theologians and all the genuflecting of a billion Christian knees, those alive today and those interred since the nights of the catacombs, could not wash away the Jewish blood that is on Christian hands. If Christ came to earth today, He would shrink from the Gothic cathedrals and the forest of church spires that carry the cross He took upon Himself that man might live a loving creature. Perhaps He would slink away to some little ghetto street in

New York City, where there is a tiny ten-by-ten synagogue. And He would sit down with the other bearded Jews on the hard benches in this true house of worship. And He would read with the others from the ancient book of Moses, which, as He said, he came to fulfill and not to destroy—the book of Moses, written in the script He could understand, written in the spirit which He lived and for which He died.

But the world will never be forgiven for anti-Semitism and what it has done to the people of the Lord, because "All your sins will be forgiven, but not the sin against the Holy Ghost."

# Learning of the Heart

THE AVERAGE HUMAN LACKS NOT KNOWLEDGE OF
the distinction between right and wrong, but
rather the will to do right by others; he well is
aware of what is right by himself, for without that
awareness he could scarcely exist. To do right by
oneself is innate in man; to do right by others—
thereon hangs the issue.

To risk danger in order to help a distressed fellow being is contrary to self-interest. To solicit
assistance from others for the distressed requires
a state of heart better than indifferent.

At no time does a sane man lack intelligence as
to right or wrong, or good or evil, with relation to
other beings. What he lacks is not intelligence but
a sympathetic state of heart.

The serious student of history will therefore
hardly find it surprising that the most vicious
deeds of evil were perpetrated not by ignorant
but rather by well educated nations. The Romans,
for instance, undoubtedly among the best edu-

cated people of late antiquity, were the greatest
evil-doers of their time. They cruelly enslaved and
exploited the natives of their subjugated provinces
and amused themselves on the sloping hills of
Rome as well as in other centers with scorpionic
forms of arena entertainment, such as unleashing
wild animals upon humans armed only with toy
weapons. In modern times, the Germans, called
the people of the thinkers and poets, launched a
program of revolting carnage that transformed all
of Europe into a Roman arena until it was stopped
by the military forces of the extra-European
world.

No one can deny that the Romans, as well as
the Germans, knew well what was right and what
was wrong, and if they did not, scarcely any other
nation ever will, for both had reached pretty much
the peak of contemporary cultural development.
The Romans were conversant with philosophical,
religious and sociological theories, and they were
tolerably up on the dogmas of the pagan as well
as the Christian faiths.

What those nations were short of was not knowledge or education, but rather character.

A study of those two nations, as well as a study

of many individuals, may show that the most erudite absorption of religion and sociology will not necessarily influence human behavior in the direction of the good. *Ex natura*, man knows what is good or bad for himself as well as his fellow men. Without this knowledge he could not have lasted as long as he has. Awareness of the rituals of religion and the laws of civics may improve his fund of information, but it will in no way change the state of his heart. And it is the heart not the mind that harbors the springs of human action.

To come back to the people of the thinkers and poets, the Teutons, to wit. The most ardent fore-runners of Nazism and Fascism were philoso-phers, Christian theologians and sociologists. The notorious Martin Niemoeller, who later laid claim to martyric incarceration, was for five years a vol-untary and direct follower of Adolf Hitler. Al-though in later years Niemoeller fell out with his gang leader, the majority of the German Christian theologians never refused to work under the direct Nazi church agents of Adolf Hitler and as willingly blessed his pirate army and arms as did the Roman priests in the days of Jupiter, Neptune and Mars. As to the German scholars, philosophers, sociologists and other men of the mind, I can only say that of those who opposed the Hitlerian ethnical nightmare, there were so few that even had they attempted to raise their voices, they would have been completely drowned out by the millions of active pro-Hitler throats grown hoarse with "Heils!" for the beloved Fuehrer. The universities of Germany stank of Hitlerism. And from all the reports that come to us, I venture to say that even today they have an odor that irks pestiferously in the nostrils of any right-hearted man or woman.

One need not be learned in the head to do the right thing, but rather learned in the heart. The learning of the heart is the most neglected branch of education today. The schools leave it to the churches and the churches leave it to the home, and whose home is the proper place for character education? Those homes that begin the morning with the receipt of dirty gossip sheets that come across the threshold only to be followed during the day by radio scripts of fiendishly contrived murder stories, silly slapstick comedies that are as tasteless as the televised bouts of ape-like men in wrestling performances. There are, of course, many other means of character education that one may find in those homes. There are dozens of pieces of youth literature, called funny and comic, which by their very examples are wantonly horrid. There is the movie in the home and in the street, bringing hold-up men and racketeers so sympathetically alive and close to the minds of the young that from there crime might easily wander to the juvenile heart.

And so it is. If the young are to learn by example, there is little they can find in the best-selling books and movies and funnies and radio scripts and television shows that will lead them to a path different from and better than that of their elders. And if we were to confess, if this whole Western Christian world were to confess as one, our sins would be so great and so numerous and so bitter as to shock the ear of the most patient Father Confessor.

To do right by others has to be taught with the same eagerness and persistence as we teach the young to do wrong by our acts of selfishness, prejudice and greed. We cannot lead a life of evil and expect good to grow out of its barrenness. Sprinkling knowledge and religious ceremony on the evil will not transform the seed. The teaching of character, a most important job, is a task forgotten.

How can the young grow to be kind to the weaker if they watch us humiliate and push down our Negro neighbors at home, at school and even in church? How can the young grow to have faith in God and the Saints if by our deeds and words we teach them to hate the Jew from whose people the Lord chose His son and His son chose His apostles? And if you strike a Jew today, you may be smiting the offspring of one of the four brothers of Christ, children of Mary, the Jewess of Nazareth!

How can the young grow to be generous of heart if you poison their minds with fables of success and fill them with greed for money conquest and job conquest and business conquest? Love for success is a poor faith to live by. Many an ugly deed had its root there, and rarely was a good one done for its sake.

How can the young grow to be kind of heart if you hang your hopes and desires on tinsel and show designed to make the gullible envious and you the core of their envy? You cannot grow fat on the envy of those you have surpassed and hope that the young will rise to loftier heights. The weight of your greed and personal ambitions will forever be a drag on the wings of the young.

The heart can learn only from another heart. The printed word does not teach it. Neither will admonitions do. Only a heart can teach a heart.

Rabbi Hillel, the ancient Israelite, once said, "The all of the law of conduct is 'What you do not wish the other to do to you, do not do it to him.'" And this sage also said, "If I do not do it, who will? And if not now, then when?"

In these few words lies perhaps the essence of human ethics. Do not do to others what you do not wish done to yourself. And begin by yourself and begin now. It is never too late to start on the path of righteousness, and the road to evil will always be only a step away.

# Science Off the Tracks

THE ROLE OF SCIENCE IN HUMAN SOCIETY IS SIMILAR to that of a stick in the hands of a hiker. The stick may be used to help the hiker along his journey. It may be used to cut down weeds or to break a path; and it may be used to bludgeon a passer-by to death. The stick has nothing to say about it. And what does the stick know about the intentions of the fist that wields it?

This most unfortunate tool relationship between science and government has given the former considerable importance in the eyes of the latter. One example of this kind of appreciation of science we find in the tragic execution of Lavoisier by the French Revolutionaries, who then regretfully put the scientist's co-workers in charge of explosives manufacture. Since the days of Lavoisier the appreciation of science has increased, and it is safe to say that during the last decade practical scientists in totalitarian governments have enjoyed a social status almost equal to that of the cream of oli-

garchic society, such as actors, political editorial-
ists, court portraitists, radio propagandists, heads of
secret police and government-friendly novelists.
In dictatorial states the practical scientist has become part-and-parcel of the camarilla that dams
up the thinking of a bewildered but powerful
populace. It is only logical for sincerely democratic governments to resort to somewhat similar
setups as a means of self-protection. And, here,
too, we begin to find the practical scientists keeping company with the upper military and propaganda crust.

I say practical scientists because there are still
some scientists who bring forth only words, and
these, as we all know, can break no bones. These
scholars continue their obscure miserable existence as philologists, philosophers, and such like.
Those, however, who deal with sticks and stones
(physicists, geologists, chemists) in their bone-
breaking field float steadily to the top like heated
air.

Science began with a gadget and a trick. The
gadget was the wheel; the trick was fire. Both existed in nature. Both certainly had been observed

by man for tens of thousands of years. As was the case with many other obvious tools of nature, man seems to have declined to apply them until he began to live in larger communities. I feel that no factor was stronger in intensifying man's inventive power than the sudden change to community living, brought about undoubtedly by some great disaster of nature. The contact of mind with mind, the matching of experience with experience, was responsible for the first simple discoveries of primitive man. These little experiences, such as seeing a dropping flint strike a spark, or a flat round stone rolled down a hill, would have been lost—as they had previously—upon an individual primitive man inhabiting a lonely cave or a brush shelter in the woods. Unless they could be transmitted to others and a use found for them, they would have been forgotten with their discoverers.

The Chinese had known explosive powder for at least a thousand years before the Western world became aware of it. But they didn't think it could be used as anything but an ingredient for firecrackers. To embed metal pieces in the powder and hurl them against people appeared to them too gruesome to conceive. Leonardo da Vinci and lesser known thinkers of the Renaissance and post-Renaissance toyed with ideas of tremendous air and water power, but they could find no use for it. And they remained chimeric ideas until economic conditions called for them. We have found in isolated countries of ancient times some very clever and intelligent gadgets which could have been of great help to other areas and continents of that time. The lack of adequate communication of information kept knowledge isolated. And finally, much that individuals knew in medicine, physics, astronomy, geography, and other branches of science in various epochs of known and unknown history was kept to themselves either out of fear of persecution or because of the indifference of their particular environment towards "useless" information.

We have come a long way from the two-wheel cart to the round-the-world transport plane, or from the sparking flint to man-made nuclear fission. Yet I wonder whether the inhabitants of Hiroshima were more aware of the evolution of science than ancient man facing an on-storming battle chariot.

Granting the many comforts and even cures that science has given man, the question still remains unanswered whether all these conveniences atone for the enduring servility of science to war-bound tyrants and their cliques. It would be in order to reconsider the value of science in the light of the foregoing, as the sinister potentialities of science increase with its progress, unless they can be harnessed by a world government. Perhaps science has harnessed enough of the powers of nature; let us now harness the powers of science.

# The Crime of Punishment

IF SOCIETY MAY BE LIKENED TO A MAN, ITS INSTITU-
tions, like the organs of a man, may be of different
ages. Some may be fresh and young, others, worn
out and almost useless. A man may have young
ears but old eyes, a good heart but a diseased
stomach. So with society. Some of our laws may
be young and true to reason, while on the other
hand our ideas of judgment and punishment may
be fossilized. We still throw offenders into pits
and cages; and the chain gangs of Georgia are
scarcely an improvement over the Bastille, except
that now we have more prisoners to keep each
other company and for a longer time.

I wonder who thought up the formula that
throwing together lawbreakers and evildoers will
purify the criminal mind. The great majority of
our caged-in citizens are adolescents and other
youthful knights of disgrace. To elect those who
have erred and mass them with other moral
failures, some of whom are repeaters with malig-

nant instincts, is more an act of evasion than one of justice. How can one hope to improve the sense of social responsibility of a youthful offender by making him spend years and years in the exclusive company of other offenders? One ought rather to assume that daily association with criminal minds will harden and deepen existing negative tendencies and the dislike and distrust of surrounding social institutions.

Criminality is an infectious disease and herding together its victims is more likely to intensify the illness and tend to create crime plagues or crime waves, than to bring forth a cure. There is perhaps no all-curing serum for criminality or any other disease, but the packing together of criminals of all types and ages into a cage-dominant communal life is little different from the dungeon system of medieval eras. The toilet facilities are more sanitary, and the diet is more balanced, but the principle is the same. After years of intimate living together with criminals, the offender walks out of the jail gates, not a better and kinder, but just a "wised up" person. To be sure, there are certain offenders who should be eliminated from society, and little does it matter what happens to them—

persons with biologically criminal instincts and violent tendencies so deeply ingrained in their sadistic minds that they can no longer be considered normal human beings and ought to be confined for life in heavily guarded penal colonies. These are the Capones and other ruthless mass killers, sex maniacs, pathological rapists, murderous assailants towards whom, unfortunately, the law has shown a peculiar leniency which, in almost every instance, has brought about a repetition of the offense. Our city streets are infested with vicious sex aggressors who are sent to jail for a year or two, readmitted again and again into society and given their freedom, which they use only to commit other atrocities. A glance at the police records of any large city will evidence this simple fact about sex offenders, whose tendencies are not based upon occasional economic conditioning or environmental causes, but are deeply involved with their very guts and glands and diseased brains, making their own lives as much the victims of their vitriolic urges as the women and children upon whom they vent their attacks.

They cannot help being repeat offenders. They

will commit their crimes as long as they live, and for their sakes as well as for the sake of the communities which they terrorize, it is best that they be removed for the rest of their lives, like other criminally insane.

It is indicative of our ridiculous establishments for punishment that recently, in the state of New Jersey, a poor widow with four children who was the beneficiary of certain state charities was convicted to serve a period of not less than five years in the state penitentiary for failing to report some meager earnings from odd cleaning jobs which augmented the small allowance she received from the state. That same week, in the same state, a vicious sex offender who had kidnapped and held captive an eleven-year-old girl for many months was given a sentence of one year. This, in spite of the fact that he had on five previous occasions been indicted for similar offenses. How will five years of living with criminals improve the social ethics of the poor widow, and in what way will the one year caging of a sexually insane man redirect his animalistic tendencies towards the normal? The criminally insane had better be removed for lifetime from normal society, while the lawbreakers of normal mind should be given a way of returning to normalcy.

The book of law of the ancient Hebrews set aside six towns as an asylum for those who broke the law. In a way, the law-breakers selected their own asylum by fleeing to one of these three towns, where they could not be apprehended. Living there was punishment enough for a normal man. Perhaps we should follow suit and set aside villages or towns of banishment where offenders would be compelled to live, but allowed to live a normal life. Our jails of today, with their sex separation, clown suits for the inmates, reform school regulations ill-adapted for the inmates' minds, dummy work programs, not much better than breaking rocks in Roman chain gangs, are a travesty on justice and certainly on social progress. What becomes of a normal man, living for one, two or ten years without feminine companionship? He becomes a punk-minded pervert, or a neurotic onanist no longer fit to live normally with men or women or children.

Our jails are breeding places of sexual perversion. Create penal villages and penal towns where offenders may live, with their families, normal lives. To be compelled to live there is hard and biting punishment enough. We need have no fear that living in such towns will not be a sufficient deterrent. This argument was brought up when, hundreds of years ago, men pleaded for abolition of the practice of chaining prisoners, for abolition of the rack and other means of torture and severe punishment, for abolition of the debtors' prison, for abolition of the death penalty for stealing a cow or a chicken. There is sufficient shame in having to live in banishment in a penal town. But if a man has served in such a colony, living a normal life with his family, he will come out a chastised man, perhaps a better man, perhaps a kinder man. For he will not have been subjected to years-long sordid intimacies with criminals, many of whom may forever bear the stamp of insanity and murderous instincts. Perhaps some day our sword of justice will be tempered with wisdom instead of with vengeance.

# History in Full Dress

HISTORY IS THE RECORDED MEMORY OF EVENTS
gone by. As such it travels on multiple levels,
levels of research interest and levels of vested
interest. And looking at our records it almost
seems that the first has become the handmaiden
of the second. Our books of history give elaborate
and detailed descriptions of what occurred on the
level of imperial conquest, princely court life, and
political usurpations. There are more details available concerning some aristocratic feud that took
place a thousand years ago than there are on the
life and problems and habits of a hundred million
little people of that era.

What matters it what king poisoned what
brother to usurp what throne, or what battle was
fought in whose favor on the road to feudal lord-
ship, or what king made his subjects allege fealty
to Rome or to himself as a self-appointed church
head? In some measure, that, too, is history.
Judged by the standards and the perspectives of

princes of the battlefield and the church, these are matters of import.

But history travels on many levels and the levels of interest to us are at considerable variance with military, court and church gossip.

We care less about the murderous intrigues of lusty Messalina than about the everyday life of Italy's men and women, working the fields and wielding the hammer of Caesarian Rome.

We care less about the diplomatic chicaneries of the saint-blessing, man-killing courtiers of medieval Europe than we do about the homes and the hearts of the tillers, the artisans and the burghers living in fear and repression under their wanton rulers.

We care less about the titled victories, the cunning and astuteness of Lord Nelson, than about the miserable fate of a thousand black souls in a thousand black ships rotting in dark, damp holds on their voyages to enslavement. I can smell the stench of the chained bodies, I can feel the anguish twisting their bewildered faces, and I can hear the moaning of their maltreated souls which dulls my senses to the fancy dress gavotte and grandeur at Buckingham Palace.

History travels on many levels. Sometimes I wish I could tear aside the levels of military and political authoritarianism so that we may see, for all the world to know, the torturous record of the past, long and forgotten, of mere man.

I see the Roman armies traversing the length and breadth of Europe, West Asia and North Africa, man-hunting and tax-hunting and land-hunting, destroying temples and shrines and dwellings. I see the little people of a whole era of a whole hemisphere made to crawl under the yoke of arrogant dictators and hypocritical senators. I see these conquered nations distributed among the Roman patricians like looted cattle—homeless, rightless, de-humanized.

And then I fail to see the glory that was Rome, and I see the ignominy that was Rome and I care little to watch the strutting of the Roman pirates through the Forum. I care little to view the statues erected to the memory of the most ruthless and most accomplished swordsmen of that gold-borne empire. And when I envisage their grandiose arenas, I do not see the purple and damask robes and the Egyptian sandals of that blood-thirstiest of nobilities; my eyes see only the terror, my ears hear only the whimper, and my nose smells only the biting odor of the sweat of fear that emanates from the sacrificial bodies of those whose last hours of living and last minutes of dying were dedicated to the surface pleasure of the sweet scented members of the Roman upper class. And in that unique perversion of morals, the victims were made to thank their executioners. *Morituri te salutant.*

Let the pages dedicated to the glorification of Roman conquests be cut from the book of history, and may the ink that was spilled in its writing run back and evaporate into just one blood-red drop, enough to write that one brief sentence: *pereat imperium.* And may a better hand fill the blank pages of history, giving its lucidness and compassion to the simple but tragic lives of the people of that hemisphere who were made to suffer the scorpions of the oppressor.

What drama there must have been in the million lives of the people wandering at the point of the Roman spear from the four corners of the globe—from the mountains of Atlas, the valley of the Nile, the plains of the Iberian peninsula, the forests of Gaul, the cold north of Britain, and the hills of Jerusalem. History travels on many levels and that was the level upon which the little people of the world traveled, a level scarcely ever remembered. And in the face of the fate of these people, in the face of true history, what peculiar idolators would care to devote time, attention and space to a rendition and glorification of how the beast ruled over man.

Throughout history I see a gilt-edged picture-book of romanticized kingdoms and duchies and townships with their castles, magnificent court affairs, perfumed codes of ethics that touch only their own kind, illustrious covenants, conclaves and concordats, campaigns and treaties; and all this I see against a background of sculptors, artists and poets at the feet of banqueteering aristocrats, while science, philosophy and theology lead a submissive existence of servitude. All these paintings and all these statues and all these poems and all these philosophical and theological servants are aligned in kowtowing before knights of the armor, and the boudoir and the king's chamber. Is that history? Is that true history?

And on the other hand we have millions of men and women, half of them tied by threat of the rack to perennial serfdom in unpaid labor to the lord of the manor, the other half living in impoverished servitude for a meager pittance with no honor or security but that which the whim of the lord bestows upon them. There was no real property that they could acquire or hold. Their homes and possessions and very lives were at the mercy of those few whom selfishly designed traditions and conspiring churches confirmed and upheld in their misdeeds, which ranked from simple murder to legalized rape. If it is true that the angels cry over every deed of evil perpetrated on this earth, if their tears were as plentiful as the rains that have fallen on us during all these centuries, they could not have washed away the filth and the blood and the sweat of misery which our historical personages have brought upon the poor and the many living in their realms.

On the lives of the oppressors in history there should be only one brief note identifying their tenebrous existence; the rest of it, with castle, equestrian statue, fancy dress with crown and mace and bloody sword, ought to go into a black book of man's misdoing to man. And let the books of true history be filled with hearty tales and pitiful songs and social understanding, searching for the life and work and suffering of the little people whose memory is all but buried beneath the showy tinsel of their malefactors.

# Humility, the Devil's Grace

HUMILITY IS ONE OF THE MAJOR SOCIAL CRIMES cultivated by the average man and woman. It is a crime because it contributes greatly to the domination by tyrannical individuals over the people at large. Docile submission to the prevailing set-up can scarcely be classified as anything but a criminal attitude.

As far back as our historical memory goes, swaggering and conniving egocentrics have made it a cardinal principle in their travels to the top to have the masses listen to and accept the fable that good men stay in their stanchions and only sinners break away into the hills.

Religious as well as political and capitalistic climbers, sometimes together, sometimes alone, have never ceased to preach, print and disseminate multiple sermons on humility for the man of the street. Not the least of their reasons for such sermons was the desire to keep the man in the street where he was and away from their purple mansions and glories. Humility is the initial grace in the carefully nurtured philosophies of those who prefer the public harmlessly on its knees, while they themselves partake to their full of the delicacies of Olympus.

Some make a fetish of humility. They are almost arrogant about it. One is almost inclined to say that they are bragging with their humility, as some do with costly possessions. This type of humility is to be found among religious opportunists who firmly believe that by foregoing certain desires here, in this temporary existence, they will obtain considerable comforts in the endlessly long hereafter. They are indeed purchasing a long-term pleasurable after-life existence with a short-term sacrifice of amoral ambitions. The morality or amorality of those ambitions for self-assertion is, of course, determined by the powers that be. So powerful may become the greed for everlasting *post mortem* paradise that those struck by this bewitching fancy may castigate, flagellate and prostrate themselves in expressions of utter humility which, as we know, is no humility at all, but rather greed to arrogate for themselves a better place in a better life.

There is a different, and true type of humility, a virtue indeed and a grace before God: It is the humility of thinking man before Thought and Verity. Such humility is an intellectual protest against the cocksureness of the superficial speaker or writer and the boisterous self-assertions of the orthodox.

In the 18th century, deep in the forests of the Carpathian Mountains, the Jewish mystic, Baal-Shem Tov, set down the principles of his revolt against orthodoxy, among which the first was *Shipluth*, humility, humility before God creative but none before the pagodas of learned tradition.

Humility before the perennial idea of *ens eterna* is of the virtues the highest. Humility of the other kind is but the teaching of self-seeking bigotry.

# Convert Jews and Convex Christians

A CONVERT JEW IS A SYMBOL OF JEWISH STRENGTH. Conversion made it possible for the faint-hearted, faithless and fear-ridden to vanish into the neighboring faiths.

Judah retains its purity. The Israelite converts are like the scum removed from the boiling soup to make it stronger and cleaner—to purify the remainder. Converts make all kinds of Christians—career Christians, escape Christians, social-climber Christians, and "let's-join-the-gang" Christians. The career Christians are willing to kneel before any idol for a seventy-five-dollar-a-week college job. The escape Christians feel that if you run like hell they may not catch you—although I hear that even in hell a "gentlemen's agreement" prevails.

The social climbers imagine that by crowding the front pews the parish priest will overlook the fact that they belong to another church. And as for those who want to be part of the big gang—

no matter how worthless and shiftless the gang may be—they are those miserable inferiority complexes who walk in fear of being recognized as Israelites, which in the eyes of the Lord is a distinction, in the eyes of the pagans a thorn, but in the eyes of these converts a blot on the surrounding all-powerful Christian world.

At the base of this convertism lies a cynical disbelief in anything but immediate opportunities, whether such opportunities offer themselves in the form of a job, an escape from persecution or discrimination, a chance to make the social register, or, by overacting the part, a chance to become one hundred percent American.

There are also, of course, those to whom sex is a factor and religion only some sort of traditional impediment. They are willing to convert whichever way the glands direct.

All these newly acquired faiths instigated by glands, salaries, salon ambition, cowardice, avarice, or plain flag-waving are no flowers in the garlands of Heavenly faith. They are just little stinkweeds.

How can a man who despises his own people have faith in Jesus Christ who pathetically upheld the teachings of Moses? How can a man who is deaf to the thunder that came from the mouths of the prophets of Israel listen to the soft whisper of a Messiah?

And if they don't believe in the miracle of the Ten Commandments, the heart of the God of Israel, before which the world stands gripped, touched, and with bended knee, how can they believe in the hundred thousand miracles performed by a hundred thousand Christified pagans?

But those converts don't believe, except in the opportunities they can grasp. And Israel is grateful to them, for by the weaklings leaving the camp Judah becomes purified.

# Literature as Merchandise

THE WORST THING THAT EVER HAPPENED TO WRIT-
ing is that it became a business. The purposes of
business are to make money, and to achieve that
end it is necessary to please as many people as possible—to amuse them, to entertain them; in short,
to do everything that will help increase the volume
of sales. Consequently, literature has been
taken over by huge business organizations—the
publishers that sell literature as others sell shoes,
television sets, or fancy hats. Experts came to the
fore, men who knew how to fabricate best sellers
and how to manufacture best selling books—people with an uncanny aptitude for detecting what
would please mob-man or mob-woman, or both.
Naturally, the literary merchandise manufactured
by these best-selling—shall we call them authors?
—accounts for the bulk of activity in the literary
market. The sale of all other books is given only
a little corner, a tiny place in the field.

We have developed an extensive group of

writers who have nothing to say but know how to say it most interestingly, people who can tell you with equal assurance what is inside Abraham Lincoln or inside the Antarctic. Some manufacturers of literature even prepare questionnaires to find out what the public would like to read, and then pick a likely author to manufacture the book according to specifications.

I think it is less important to cogitate the fact that half of America does not read any book, than it is to deplore the kind of book the other half reads. This calls to mind the saying of the rabbi who entered the home of a pagan whose shelves were filled with worthless parchment: "I see all these volumes," said the rabbi, "but I fail to see the Book." Ghost-written pseudo-autobiographies of retired generals and statesmen are not books. Vainglorious reports by loud-mouthed columnists and smart-aleck journalists about peoples and countries which they visited on blitz tours, spent mostly in planes, depots and American-style hotels —these jazzed-up write-ups are not books. Fanciful dramatizations and fictionalizations of important historic facts and figures, concocted by semi-educated facile pen-pushers are not books, no matter how artfully sex elucidations are interwoven with the historic web. Pollyanna sermons by Women's Clubs preachers are not books.

A book occurs when man experiences things of great depth and significance and feels compelled to relate his inner experiences. There are such books, written ones as well as unwritten ones. The ancient Hebrews, when they said "Book," meant the Book of Law. As the decades and centennials went by they added new writings of wisdom to the old ones, joined parchment to parchment, and they could think of no other book but the Bible, The Holy Book.

They, too, had some irrelevant scribblings by irrelevant people on irrelevant subjects, but they didn't call those papers books, because a book was a great thing, a holy thing. And so it came about that the many books of wisdom of the Hebrews were collected and put together, and are still together as *The Book*.

There are other great books. Enter your libraries. Perhaps you will find one or another stuck away somewhere amongst the thousands of items of book merchandise. Enter your bookshop. Gaze into the window. Perhaps you will find the Book among the gaudy-jacketed fabrications of our shrewd sales experts. A real book is a living thing; he who touches it, touches man himself. And all the other elegantly packaged writings of Hollywood-eyed and Book-Club-eyed typewriter entrepreneurs are just a sham and a farce, and an ugly caricature of the first man who ever sat down and cut into clay or sand some deep-felt thought or some deep-felt emotion that he wanted to share with his fellow man. Perhaps some day some Hercules will come and clean the publishers' stables of the bearded phonies and the check-suited wise-guys and make room for Pegasus.

# Glands and the Heavens

LIKE ANY ANIMAL OF LIVING TISSUES, MAN IS SUB-
ject to innumerable sensual impressions and desires. Man living alone would find little reason to
restrain himself or others of these until his appetite had been satiated or other stronger desires had
succeeded in directing elsewhere the cravings of
the body.

There have been some students of human
nature to whom man appeared as an animated
machine stimulated by sensual impulses and
driven by succeeding desires.

Man's desires are as multiple as his impulses
and impressions, and in his natural state they are
his masters. Some early Greek philosophers tried
vainly to assign human emotions and desires, as
well as ideas, to definite parts of the body. For
some reason they seated thought in the heart and
desire in the stomach. Some Talmudists attributed
a wandering existence to the human emotions and
desires, maintaining that they all started in the

head whence they traveled to the heart and from there to the lower regions. For that reason, of course, the Talmudists were very severe with persons thinking wrong thoughts; once the wrong has nested in the mind, it is bound to make the rest of the journey.

I think that desires are not confined by anatomy nor by restrictions. Desires are body itself and body can live as little without them as a river can without flowing or the wind stop blowing.

Some religious schools and cults have attempted to dam up the senses. Such teachings are based on ignorance of the natural functions of the senses. In many instances the practice of damming up desires is based on little more than mis-reading of some ancient sayings or writing.

The desire to eat pork is a cardinal offense to a Moslem, while it is a pastime with the Christian world. On the other hand, the drinking of alcoholic beverages is devilish to a Moslem, a delight to the Hebrew, and not less with the Christian. Furthermore, the Moslem considers it proper enjoyment to conduct organized marriage with a herd of women, while to the Christian this appears an outrage; indeed, the old Christian church requires of its priests a celibate existence.

Such a monastic existence is also in favor with the Buddhists and Hindus, who deem it devilish to butcher and devour animals, a form of activity considered part of the good life in the Christian world.

As the foregoing indicates, the limitations set upon the sensual life are generally determined by some ancient tradition rather than by ethical considerations.

Clergymen who would benignly bless the bayonets and hand grenades of the Austrian or German war-lords will irately censure a member partaking of fowl on Friday or the common-law living of a harmless couple.

I am rather inclined to think that the beaming countenance of a war-blessing clergyman is a far greater abomination in the eyes of the good Lord than the personal sex life of Jack and Jane, no matter how unconventional their sanctions.

If there are ethics that find pleasure in the mind of the Lord, they are not based, I am sure, on pork or whiskey, fasting or sex glands. What cheap morals must these be that are founded on such trifling matters, and how childishly these clergy-men blind-fold themselves against the glare of the bloody senses that rave.

Do they think that minorities have no voice in heaven? Do they think the Lord will never lend His ear to the black man and listen to his tale of woe? Do they think the Lord knows no Hebrew, or has no heart for the suffering of His first people? If this were so, why would He choose an African, born and raised on the Nile, to be His Prophet and Law-giver?

For thousands of years, the persons in power, together with their churches, have ground their heels on the small man, kept him in misery and contempt. The rulers of Europe, until a few generations ago, had the farmer tied to his shack and plow, like a team of oxen, and left him only enough of soddy grub and bleak shelter to keep skin and bones together. In sections of Christian Germany, their ethics even gave the lord of the manor the *jus primae noctis*, the right to the first night with every bride in the county.

In other sections similar rights were taken and tolerated by the powers that were and the churches that stood.

In our own country, for hundreds of years, neighbors black of skin, though Christian of confession, were dealt with like cattle: men sold on the open market, weighed and prodded as horses would be, by their buyers; women exposed half-naked and naked to the highest bidder. That wasn't 5000 years ago, but a few memory rounds back when your grandfather went to church and listened to grand, eloquent sermons on how to cork up your glands, your whiskey, and your swear words.

Reason and common-sense are strong enough to curb the want for food, and wine, and love-life. There is a far greater need to curb the lust for the suppression and humiliation of man, than the thirst of the senses for their trifling satiations. And if the nostrils of the Lord are offended by the untidy cravings of the body, the bestiality of the Dominant against the Weak is a stench to Him that all the myrrh and all the incense of the church cannot eradicate.

# Proverbs and Profits

THE STAMP OF IMMORALITY IS SET UPON A THING
or an action by a governing individual with ul-
terior motives, sometimes a corporate individual,
more often mere tyrannical man. As the law of
taboo is not a natural law but one imposed upon
the community under an aegis, taboos differ as
rulers differ.

In our Western countries, business magnates
or generals would be spurned as outcasts were
they to bring into their married household a score
of ravishing concubines, while in Peking or
Shanghai, for instance, accomplished leaders of
society would not hide such consorts from the eyes
of the public. In still a third country Gandhi, the
prophet of one-fifth of the human race, would
have marked taboo monogamy as well as polyg-
amy, espousing the virtue of celibacy.

Many Christian teachers and churches have
held taboo the depositing of sperm in the female.
Some of the Hindu as well as Christian moralists

reckon that man loses virtue with his semen and gains in holiness with continence. Still, this sex taboo has its peculiarities. While on the one hand persons of good society would hardly find it proper to discuss in the parlor the manner of their sperm emissions as one discusses a dinner or an operation, the churches as well as the people of India—no less than in the Christian countries—seem to have lifted the taboo against *materia sexualis* as it pertains to weddings.

Marriage, or the binding together of two people of opposite sex in the comradeship of living together, is rarely celebrated as a weighty contract affecting the whole life of two intimate persons, but rather as a prospective orgy. Instead of being witnesses at a solemn meeting, appropriate for such an occasion, the eyes and the minds of those around the couple leer at the forthcoming consummation of a sexual act, from which the usual taboo has been temporarily lifted. And the honeymoon increasingly takes on the aspects of a publicly sponsored orgy. These customary sex-emphasized honeymoons with their inevitable disillusionments have a large stake in the making of a neurotic attitude towards marriage, with its accent on animalistic satisfaction.

Some of the most remarkable taboos originated in feudal times, supported no less by the lawmakers, the lords, than by the law-protectors, the Churches. The natural desire for comfort, property and security became taboo. The lords of Europe had neither the wish nor the religion to have the common people share in their wealth. To keep the masses of Europe quiet under the chains of suppression, the masters of their fate created an intricate web of taboos, the remnants of which can still be found in our society. It became immoral to wish for fine clothes or fine homes or rich food or to worry about tomorrow. And here is the Because:—because the Lord was poor and the Lord takes care of the birds in the fields, and it is not Christian to desire these things, and before all, be meek, because the meek will inherit the earth and the last will be first. Out of the wealth of the Hebrew wisdom literature, including those sections of the New Testament which stemmed from the same Hebraic mind, the callous Europeans wove a vicious spider web of taboos which kept the Western World in darkness for almost two thousand years. In our proverbs you will still find traces of the pretty sayings and pretty prohibitions to which the people of Europe were subjected during that era.

They made the masses work seventy and eighty hours a week, under the pretty proverb, "Work never killed anybody." They had no use for workers in the dark evenings, so they taught them "Early to bed and early to rise." They wanted them to live on the pittance of their pay, so they taught them, "Waste not, want not." They wanted them never to rest, they wanted them never to think, so they taught them "Idle hands bring mischief" and "Too much thinking makes you sick."

They had a world of taboos and every taboo was another link in the chain to hold down the common people of Europe, to rob them of everything they had and to keep the impoverished satisfied with their poor lot with hopes for the Hereafter.

The lords of Europe paid off the slaves of Europe with immortality, a cheap currency indeed, while they themselves pursued their Lucullian manner of living in sumptuous palaces built with the same blood and sweat and terror as their grandiose cathedrals. But each of those points as an accusing finger to the heavens, crying out the insufferable hardship and ugliness which was laid upon the common people to bring about their erection.

# Objectors Without Conscience

WHERE TYRANNY EXISTS, TO SIT AT PEACE IS A crime. War, any war, is, true enough, a "sin of hell," but often there is no other way of burying hell on earth except by war.

More frequently than not, the conscientious objector is a man without a conscience. It troubles him little that the German Hitler hordes terrorized and massacred the flower of Europe so long as he himself may be left undisturbed in his dreamy existence on the far-away island of America. The conscientious objector to war is like that tender-hearted passerby whose only reaction to a cruel child-beater would be to run to the nearest analyst or the nearest church to try to forget all about it. The conscientious objector does not wish to help the grieved, the attacked, the suppressed. He is annoyed and afraid of the responsibility and dangers that wars are fraught with, but instead of putting up the white sheet of surrender to the enemy, he hoists the flag of an allegedly white conscience. He objects on religious grounds. He objects to what? Not to the murderous onslaught by the tyrant and his henchmen upon a peaceful people. Nay, his conscience is pregnant with divine objections—objections to being drafted by solidarity-minded citizens to fight a vicious enemy.

The conscientious objector has a peculiar set of senses. He doesn't hear the whimpering of the women and children being tortured, gassed and buried in German concentration camps. His eardrums are like those of a dog who fails to grasp a pitch that we can hear, but are attuned to some other acoustic vibration we cannot perceive. The cries of the martyred do not strike the eardrums of the objector; he seems to be listening devotedly to some celestial tunes of peaceful bliss.

His sight, too, is much like that of a dog. The conscientious objector just doesn't see the red color of the blood on the hands of the usurper's henchmen. Everything appears to him in a hazy, greyish blue, serene and unperturbed.

Under the cloak of religious conviction, the conscientious objector hides his own little greedy pot of isolated consummation. He will not share with others the bread of living. "Let them perish," his thoughts wander, as long as he can live out his life in what we consider miserable but he deems canny separation.

The prophets of religion never condoned acquiescence to evil, but rather immortalized the undaunted war against enslavers. "I did not come to bring peace, but rather the sword." The monuments in the literature of the God-intoxicated were not placed to the memory of the cowardly escapists but to those who lived, fought and perished in the valor of battle. From the deeds of Joshua to those of Judah Maccabee and Bar Kochba; from the deeds of the blind Samson to the Unknown Soldier cut down by a German bullet; from the time of Spartacus down to Abraham Lincoln the war of conscience has stood in awe before the sword of the soldier for righteousness—that conscience which the objector lost, and now he cannot see the eternal flame of human freedom streaming into the skies from the point of the sword.

# The School of Submission

IF FREEDOM IN DEMOCRACY BE THE CORRECT EXPRES-
sion of man's political life, why then do so many
people obviously choose to live without and outside democracy? To this, I can answer only that
man is like a wild horse, loving its freedom; but
man can also be captured and corralled, thus be-
coming, by sweet words as well as by the whip,
the beast of burden for his captors.

As in many other matters concerning basic
tendencies in man, we have to seek not for one
motive, but for a group of them.

Not one cause accounts for man's submission,
voluntary submission, to tyranny—but many are
the causes. There is early religious training with
its teaching of submission to an abstract deity.
(And with what frequency have tyrants pressed
such theological abstractions into their devious
service, thus making the Lord a henchman of the
devil.) Then there are the rather rigid and disciplinarian methods of education practiced in so

many schools of the European continent and the Asiatic hemisphere. These methods create in the child an almost blind obedience to teacher and parent alike, and inculcate a worship of authority accompanied by subservience to superiors, teachings which impress themselves indelibly on young minds. And from the symbolic *"Render unto Caesar that which is Caesar's,"* grows a respectfulness with respect to Caesar that permits the Caesars, little and large, to take from the flock not only the wool but also the hide.

The political infantilism of man that crops up from one corner of the globe to another is, in a way, nothing but the reversal of man to childhood. We see grown men foregoing their rights to vote, their rights to free speech, their rights to the free pursuit of happiness and voluntarily placing themselves inside the barbed wire corrals of callous political bosses. Of course, in addition to the psychological motivation created by the weaknesses of pseudo-religious education and a disciplinarian school and home-life which makes grown-ups yearn for the protective cage of living by obedience instead of free choice—in addition to these we face here the effects of an open and brutal terrorizátion of people's minds by conniving tyrants. These systematic terror tactics have proven most effective. Purposefully, brutalities are practiced openly and in violation of all human rights and religious principles. The purpose is to instill panic and fear into the wide masses, since fear is the tyrant's most powerful weapon. Once this fear has gripped a people already weakened by a discipline-ridden childhood, they collapse into shivering jelly, spineless, heartless, and forever in fear.

And since fear is the twin-sister of cowardice we find the great blubber man ready to stamp out even the trace of freedom at the behest of the booted man with the whip. The boot more than anything else, perhaps, symbolizes in our time the submission of man to nefarious oppressors. In our day we have seen scholars and scientists, artists and educators, bow deeply before the boot, for such is human nature that a cat-o'-nine-tails can make of freedom-loving natural man a slimy vicious groveling creature fearful of the world.

Free men have no right to live and work in isolation if they wish to retain the bliss of their heritage. Rather is it their duty to crash into the lairs of the slave-makers and slave-holders, so that the rest of the world may become free and stay free.

Less than two hundred years ago the people on this continent began the march toward freedom. They lit this torch; the French picked it up and held it until Napoleon wrested it from their hands, but freedom was on the march. There are still a thousand obstacles in the way of freedom. Perhaps the people of this continent will finish what they began—to make the people free, and make certain they stay free.

# The Orators and the Yoke

DEMOCRACY IS THE ONLY CORRECT AND ENLIGHT-
ened concept of man's true position in society. By
recognizing his duties towards the community, as
well as the privileges due him from the community, man becomes an intelligent member of
society.

The earliest known forms of this philosophy and
form of government are to be found among the
ancient Hebrews, and later among the Greeks.
Some historians have on occasion confused ancient
types of sovereign-centered communism and
totalitarianism, such as that practiced, for instance,
by the Incas, with democracy. However, even the
most benevolent and patriarchal tyrannies are
still tyrannies.

Tyrannies have almost always used patriarchal,
religious and socialistic terminology in their efforts
to control the masses. The Japanese Mikado
would have his Shinto theologians divine his
celestial origin, a device not much different from

that used by the Pharaohs of Egypt or Montezuma of the Aztecs, and Hitler would studiously
sprinkle his imperialist nationalism with socialist
phraseology, just as fraudulent as the welfare
corporate state of Mussolini's fascism.

Patriarchal, socialistic, or religious emotionalism
has always been a prerequisite to the establish-
ment and retention of tyrannical government. To
confuse the simple proposition that free man is
the master of his own fate, with a free voice, a free
vote, and the right to cooperate with his fellow
man—to confuse this basic truism concerning
*anthropos* and *polis*, the tyrant has to create absolutistic abstractions such as "fatherland," "divine
heritage," "race purity" to which the average man
must sacrifice his voice, vote, and freedom. These
abstractions, be they religious, patriarchal, or socialist, are cleverly designed to deprive the individual of his clear political thinking and enmesh
him by threats, terror, and persuasion in the net
of pseudo-political fabrications, so that as time
goes by men lose sight of the true paths of the
mind, and become lost completely in the blind
alleys of totalitarianism.

So great is the cunning of tyrannical propaganda

that we may find in only a brief decade or two that the subjects of such tyrannical governments consider it the most wholesome way of life for man to live—like an imbecile or a child completely in obedience to one man and his clique, accepting enthusiastically such ridiculous tokens of political self-deception as voting in a one-ticket election. These utterly confused subjects, who have access only to official censored propaganda information, eye pitifully those peoples who suffer under the stress of democratic government with its freedom of press, freedom of personal travel and communication, and freedom to vote and be voted for.

It is because of these frailties of the human mind that the people who live under true democracy become militant and drive the tyrants off the platforms from which they harangue, befuddle, and spellbind a neighboring people.

# Schadenfreude

THIS IS A GERMAN WORD MEANING "PLEASURE FROM the suffering of others." The word has no equivalent in our language. Not that some Americans do not become on occasion *schadenfreudig*. But so rare is this mental aberration among our people that we did not find it necessary to coin a word for it.

*Schadenfreude* is not lust at the pain of a fellow man. It is not a sadistic emotion and therefore a subject for psychiatric analysis, but rather a kind of intellectual glee at the misfortune of a fellow man. In their by now historic inferiority feeling, the Germans developed this "pleasure" to such a degree of popularity that this ugly word describing humanity's ugliest pleasure, was given a place in the language.

This education in *Schadenfreude* was abetted by the chauvinistic directives of German leaders. They developed that unbridled competitive spirit which in their consuming greed for a top place in the sun they deemed a supreme requirement. As all the millions of German strutting inferiority complexes hustled in a self-created race for achievement by subjugation, so great was the fear that they might fall behind, that the weakening or collapse of their fellow man (not excluding those of their own race) was contemplated with a sincere feeling of relief. The smirk on the face of the German school child watching another kid fail differs little from the smirk on the faces of passersby watching gleefully the torturous beating given an old Jewish woman by a Nazi Storm Trooper.

Herein lies, perhaps, the key to the understanding of the mind of modern Germany, in its revolting evolution toward social deviltry since the days of the obese conniving Prussian politician Bismarck, whom his confounded people admiringly referred to as "The Iron Chancellor." In Germany's education for *Schadenfreude* lies the answer to the riddle of how and why sixty million people permitted themselves to butcher two million Slavs and six million Jews systematically, coldly, almost peacefully one could say—peacefully as the burial in a cemetery. Sixty million Germans didn't bat an eye when endless freight cars were stuffed to suffocation with humans old and young. This unspeakable crime, of pressing a hundred women, children and broken men into a hermetically sealed car, thereby compelling parents to watch the agonizing death by suffocation of their offspring, can never be forgiven nor forgotten by civilized mankind. But it can be better understood in the knowledge of Germany's most popular emotional uplift—*Schadenfreude*. Visualize sixty million victory-intoxicated Teutons scurrying through all the corners of Europe in their hunt for defenseless Jews so they might turn them over to the authorities for extermination. In their *Schadenfreude* about the fallen Jews, or for that matter, the fallen Slavs, they hunted cellars, roofs and forests, leaving none in hiding. With inspired glints in their eyes they vied with each other for the amazing privilege of being the first to clear their towns or villages or hamlets of every living Jewish creature. Great was their *Freude* and indubitable their accomplishment. Perhaps in years to come historians will refer to the Germans of the twentieth century as the people of the *Schadenfreude*.

# You Can't Catch Up With the Past

THE CONCEPT OF INTERMARRIAGE IS BASED ON THE traditional notion persisting in the Western World that the human race divides itself biologically and spiritually into segmentary groups such as the Anglo-Saxons, the Germans, the Mediterranean peoples, the various Asiatic races, the African groups, etc.

Anthropology offers a striking example of how a little knowledge may create prejudices of gigantic proportions.

If we were to retrace in slow motion the expansion and growth of Western man (in much the same way that a film shows a diver hopping off a spring board, and then for the amusement of the audience reverses the mechanism and has him jumping from the water back up on to the board), were we to reverse the mechanism of history, we would see the white people from all over the world hustling back into Europe from the four corners of the earth, first in large streams, then in a tiny trickle, and finally the conquerors of the 15th, 16th, and 17th centuries, frequently referred to as discoverers, would sail back into the ports of the Mediterranean and the French and English coasts. By the year 1450 we would find scarcely a single Christian of the Western World engaged in the exploitation of foreign pagan races in faraway lands.

If we were to reverse the mechanism further, we now would see hundreds of thousands of Europeans traveling East across the plains of the Ukraine to the shores of the Black Sea and even as far as the tundras of Siberia and the steppes of Mongolia. We would find ourselves now in the year 1,000, prior to our era—and where is Western man? The mountains and valleys of Europe are nothing but forests inhabited by nomadic hunters and cattle-close tribesmen, with some fishermen living together for protection in shacks built on stilts on the lake shores. Only on the coasts of the Eastern Mediterranean and in the lands between the Euphrates and Tigris, among the peoples known as Sumerians, Egyptians, and Israelites, are discernible lights which in later years were to drive away some of the darkness that hovered over Europe in ancient times. It was the Greeks who carried westward this torch of the *Lux Orientalis.*

And of this spiritual fire that burned in Asia Minor three thousand and five thousand years ago, we can see only the luminous reflection; the rest of man's past is darkness and silence. Of man's one-million-year-old life story, we have become aware of only five thousand years, a fleeting moment indeed in the titanic stream of time.

How now can anyone with a fair sense of perspective and historical equity accept the arbitrary segmentation supported by Western man?

God lived with the world and its people for a million years before Christ was born, so why begin time with the Son of God? Why not with God, the Father? There must have been good and evil before Christ came to earth; there must have been sin and repentance, devotion and derision, helpfulness and viciousness, manliness and gentleness and godliness; there must have been saints and thieves, Falstaffs and ascetics, foul men and sound men, naive men and critics, the Lord's servants and the Devil's henchmen.

There was a God before Christ.

There must have been salvation and justification for a million years to a hundred million people before the Europeans began to adorn themselves with the symbol of the cross, *in hoc signo,* and set upon the other children of God to convert them and subject them and suppress them and enslave them *ad majorem dei gloriam* with fire and sword.

With the exception of the Jews, there is no group living in the Western World that has retained even a semblance of its racial heritage. The white people of the Western World have been in an endless series of migrations for the last 3,000 years. Of their origin, they know nothing beyond that it is based on a turbulent mixture with Teutons, Mongols, Huns, and Janissaries. As for the period reaching beyond the last 3,000 years, I doubt whether any Western man would care to look that far back, for he would have to search for his ancestors in the foul caves and the dense forests and swamp lands of a barbaric Europe.

To sober Western man still further, it need only be brought to his attention that to the best of our knowledge the only people who during Europe's "Wild Boar" period were enjoying the nobility of culture, religion, and the arts were the Egypto-Africans, the Jews, and other Asiatic peoples whom the men of the Western World today prefer to segregate among the bottom brackets.

Occasionally, some magnanimous Westerner has suggested intermarriage with the Jews, perhaps as a price for their elimination. A few generations ago the German philosopher Fries suggested the drowning of all new-born Jewish boy babies as a method for eliminating the Jewish problem. This would compel Jewish girls to marry into the surrounding Western races.

Forceful intermarriage or even voluntary intermarriage may eliminate the personal racial issues of those concerned, but it doesn't resolve the issue itself.

The issue is simply this: Western man knows less of his origin and background than any other major group of people. Man at large can trace the footsteps of his ancestors for only a few thousand years. To separate man from man, race from race, and people from people on the basis of our feeble intelligence of the origin and development of man is merely an expression of the arrogant desire prevailing in certain groups to be better

than other groups. In the eyes of Truth, the differences between man and man—differences in
skin pigmentation, hair texture, width of nose, the
angle at which the eyes are set, the height of the
legs—are insignificant. We do not know what happened in the million years of man's history that
resulted in these differences. It is certain, however, they did not occur to give white people the
right to rule over black people, or yellow over red,
for in the eyes of the Lord a million years are as a
day, and man is only a fleshy speck on the edges of
this globe.

# The Angels Don't Keep Pets

THE LORD MUST HAVE LOVED ANIMALS EVEN MORE
than he did poor people, because he made so many
of them. Actually, there are many more humans
ready to stand by a dog or cat than there are
humans ready to help a poor man.

Emile Zola is said to have judged people by their
attitude towards animals. I should like to reverse
this perspective, and judge lovers of animals by
their attitude towards people. Whenever I face a
man or woman paying with time, earnings and
efforts to make life comfortable for dogs or cats
or canaries or horses or parrots, I try to find out
how much this person contributes towards increas-
ing the happiness of mere human beings. It
seems odd to me, at a time when a million mouths
of a million infants are parched for lack of a glass
of milk or a slice of bread in China, India, Europe,
and even some of our own Southern states, to
throw tanks of milk and barrels of meat daily
before a million parasitic cats and dogs who do

nothing to justify their existence but gratify the frustration of certain twisted semi-adult emotionalists who like to satisfy their barren souls with the sterile satisfaction of animal love.

It is amazing how many of these dog and cat devotees would resent with open hostility any attempt to have them transfer their aberrational affections to humans. I have watched these animal fanciers with amazement as they offer their lips to the guttery muzzle of a slobbering dog that has jumped straight from an hour of manure sniffing to the benignly smiling face of its master. There are persons who joyfully smooch with a germ and flea infested bitch, but would not think of sharing a park fountain with a Negro child. I have seen women take half-a-dozen urinous cats into bed with them, women who would be horrified at the mere thought of living in the same apartment house with a Negro family.

I have often wondered why our city fathers permit the keeping of these useless animals in our crowded homes, whence they are let out three times a day to cover sidewalk and park with their defecations. Some years hence—many years, I am afraid—people will look back upon our domestic animal hobbies as being as barbarous hygienically as medieval gutters seem to us today. Our streets serve as open latrines for a million meat-eating animals to the stench of which we have become as accustomed as the medieval burgher to the human defecation in his side ditches.

Man's attitude towards the animal is, to say the least, most peculiar. Only recently the Dean of Hereford in England conducted his early services dedicated to St. Francis of Assisi (the good Saint who preached a sermon to the birds and squirrels) before forty horses, a hundred dogs and cats, rabbits and goldfish, with a goose, a cock, a snake, a canary, a goat and a tortoise in the pews. Naturally, the owners of these pets were also in attendance. I do not know what became of the horses and the goldfish. I have a feeling, however, that by now the goose and the cock and the goat have attended church for the last time. Such perverse elevation of a dumb beast is not new. In ancient Egypt the bull Apis was actually deified, and so were crocodiles and birds. Among the Hindus the belief in transmigration of the soul from man to animal makes for sanctification of even the most distasteful vermin. While some of the Hindus thought nothing of cutting up hundreds of thousands of Moslems in the recent population transfer, they would not even think of butchering a cow strolling about the market place.

It is known that some of the most vicious men in history were sublimely fond of animals. The infamous Julius Streicher, the sadistic torturer of helpless prison inmates, on his nightly homecoming, took his boots off on the threshold so as not to disturb his sleeping canary. Adolf Hitler just couldn't stand the smell of animal blood, while genocide left him howling with glee. History is full of such stark incongruities.

We can see one type of man treat the dog as a kind of natural comrade and companion of man, while the same man takes the same dog into God's beautiful forest to hunt down in a beastly manner a tender little doe, or a funny little rabbit, or a covey of pretty partridges. Why it is perfectly all right to bark down or tear down or shoot down a harmless grass-eating deer, and yet a horrible thought to eliminate flesh-devouring, foul-smelling dogs and cats, is beyond my comprehension. Incidentally, the dogs we see so ardently admired for their talent of being able to sit up and raise a paw before we throw a bleeding chunk from a cow into their throats, these same dogs are being raised in provinces of China, and were raised in some provinces of Italy, on corn and other grains, for the dinner table, just as hogs are here, which dogs most closely resemble anatomically and physiologically, even in their food habits, for both of them are carnivorous as well as herbivorous. It is also well known that some Chinese have made pets of pigs and would as soon think of butchering their pet pig as some of us would of serving Fifi or Rover for supper.

As for horses, which stand highest on our list of beloved co-creatures, the people of Vienna and other cities of middle and eastern Europe have, for many generations, been connoisseurs of horsemeat. Vienna has a considerable number of butcher shops that sell horse meat exclusively.

As we can see by looking at the past as well as at the present, the same animals that are regarded by some people as man's best friend are considered by others as man's best meal. We all remember the troubles of the Eskimo who visited his explorer friend in New York and during a brief ab-

sence of his host calmly partook of three live goldfish from the parlor bowl. He just couldn't understand his host's outrage, for only the day before
he had watched his host toss a live lobster into a
boiling pot.

What we call the love of animals is nothing but
a feeling of satisfaction—first, at being master;
second, at being provider; third, at being awaited;
fourth, at being appreciated.

What we love here is not the animal, but ourselves in the role of the receiver of gratitude,
appreciation and obedience. It is quite a sop to
self esteem—especially in persons with strong in-
hibitions and feelings of inferiority—to be able to
expend upon dumb animals natural instincts for
giving; we react enthusiastically if they can eat or
drink and will unhesitatingly obey the master
over food and shelter. The appreciation and gratitude of animals can be increased still further by
running with them or horsing around with them as
other animals would. Not only cows and horses
and dogs and cats react in this manner, but also
crocodiles and bears and lions and skunks, although most of the larger cats are inclined to act

like some of the dogs—they love only one man, the one that feeds them.

How fickle man's affection for animals really is. One can see it in the love pat a farmer gives his calf; he has the calf nuzzle up to his face, and the very next day comes to the barn with a large knife and slits the critter's throat. It is astonishing that Western man should love cats and dogs, two rat- and mouse-hungry foul-smelling beasts (the dog far outranges the cat as rat catcher), while in the deer, Nature's most attractive creature—plant-eating, gracious and kind—in this far superior animal he can see only a steak. I presume the reason for these emotional preferences lies in the fact that the deer will not grovel in the dirt to catch an easy slice of beef, for the wide meadows give it all the food it requires.

If man were to love animals he would love the sensitive deer, or the magnificent buffalo, or the elegant gazelle. These animals live without blood on their teeth—they live on the green of the prairies; they are free and look at man in shy amazement, or in fear, because man smells of the flesh and blood he has devoured.

Man doesn't love animals. He wants a slave, and the dog and the cat follow him, whine and purr and bark, and sit on their haunches, and raise their paws, and lick his fingers, and lick his face, and lick his boots—and man loves the slave. He loves himself in the role of the slave-keeper and all the frustrations and shy inferiority complexes of inhibited souls are spent on those beasts to elevate the animal-lover's puny self, not to help any creature of God, for if there is a thirst for love in the heart of man let him drink from the eternal fountain of the greater self that embraces all mankind.

There are a million yearning hearts of a million suffering children, yellow, black and white. If your chest is bursting for the want of love, the son of man is always ready to receive it, and the love you give to man and the child of man will come back a thousandfold. There is no greater satisfaction than love returned. Are your ears eager for the meow of a cat, or the bark of a dog? Would you not rather see the jubilation in the eyes of a waif whom you have taken unto yourself? Drive the dogs and cats from your door, back to their rat- and vermin-infested haunts, and take to your hearth God's little creatures, black, yellow, or white. Don't let the dog lead you on the leash; let the child take you by the hand.

So long as there is a suffering waif starving in this bitter world, it is a sin to cater to a dog.

# Sin, Sex and Sanity

ABSTINENCE CAN BE CONSIDERED A CIVILIZED VERsion of the primitive code of taboo prevalent among the aborigines. We are speaking, of course, of abstinence as a discipline of the soul, for abstinence can also be viewed as a prophylactic or a health measure or as evidence of functional antagonism or disinterest. The majority of the world's population, for instance, abstains from smoking out of sheer dislike of the sensation. A small fraction abstains for health reasons. But the orthodox Jew refrains from smoking on the Sabbath as a discipline of the soul. The majority of the people of the world refrains from drinking burgundy, having no taste for it. Some leave the wine alone in order not to impair their health. But the Moslem will not drink it as a discipline of the soul. There are some people in the world, especially among the female sex, whom sexual intercourse leaves cold. There are some who avoid it on the advice of physicians. But the ordained priest of the Christian Mother Church refrains from it as a discipline of the soul.

It is only abstinence as a discipline of the soul that touches our interest here, and as such, it is known as far back as history takes us. The code of Hammurabi, which goes back to 2000 B.C., speaks of celibate priestesses. Some of the ancient Hebrew sects, such as the Essenes, were addicted to severe asceticism. There can be no doubt that the practices of the Essenes and similar Jewish sects exercised considerable influence in creating ascetic tendencies among the early Christians, among whom such converts as the Jew Saul (St. Paul) played a dominant role. The tendency to religious monasticism (*monk* being a corruption of the Greek *living alone*) is stronger yet among the various sects in India, the Hindus as well as the Buddhists. The Chinese travelers Fa-Hsien and Hiuen Tsung report encountering in old India rich and extensive communities of "those living alone," some having as many as five thousand members. The contemporary Hindu sage Mahatma Gandhi was, in his later years, a pronounced ascetic, strongly opposed to sexual intercourse. To the question, "What would become of the human race, if all people would practice such sexual abstinence?" he replied, "God will find a way." However, the rich population growth in India, as well as among the Christian nations of Catholic Europe, indicates that the people at large, in spite of their staunch faith in their saints and sages, hesitate to put Providence to such a severe test.

There is also a philosophical kind of abstinence imposed upon the body by pure reasoning as a matter of moral health. Ascetic philosophy can be traced to the beautiful though bitter laments of King Solomon. The Solomonic sentiments on the disquieting aspects of human desires were subjected to systematic reasoning by the Stoics, especially Epictetus, Seneca and that philosopher king, Marcus Aurelius. "He who desires not will not have his life pulled hither and thither by lust and wish." "As the highest good in life is peace with one's self and peace with Nature, the wise man will gladly sacrifice his desires upon the altar of union with one's self and Nature." This thought was explored in the 17th century by Baruch Spinoza, whose *Ethics* should demonstrate how man can free himself from the shackles of desires and affectations, especially the lust for money, honor and sex (which toss people about like leaves in the wind). In the eyes of Spinoza, the free man is one who in inner awareness of himself and Nature is guided by reason and intuition, rather than by the desires of his body.

Stoic, or Spinozistic abstinence, has little in common with religious abstinence, which is our concern at this point. Religious abstinence is based on a taboo for the justification of which the theologians from the Angakok, the Eskimo Amazon land, to the modern Hindu or Buddhist adherents and the Christian monks can only give us a hint as to its divine investiture. The taboos of course differ in different religions. We might say that the taboo of sexual intercourse is strongest in the Christian Western World. Somehow it has been ingrained in the minds of the Christian people that refusing to perform sexual functions elevates man to some rung of sanctity.

So strong was this conviction in the medieval ages that the French philosopher Abélard, who was brutally castrated by the relations of his mistress, Héloise, considered himself fortunate in thus having been freed from bodily enslavement. One can readily understand that some highly self-critical persons, such as Augustine, who had lived a life of debauchery, might in later years, because of weakness, loss of capacities, or disease, begin to look upon the sex act itself as porno-deviltry. Perhaps if these men had never become slaves of their desires, emotionally perverted and over-sexed, they would have had no urge to hiss at every female as though she were Lilith, the snake woman. Without wanting to give undue credence to the bawdy tales of medieval monastics, one must say that the elimination of women from the lives of hundreds of thousands of normal young men is bound to lead to erotic confusion rather than holiness.

There is not the slightest case for the belief that man can contribute towards Godliness or human welfare by losing his semen womanless like Onan. And lose he must, as he must lose the many other juices and fluids the frail body exudes through its sweat glands, nasal membranes, lach-rymal glands, etc. No one is helped by a man's withholding his semen, and this is no plea for its misuse or squandering, but if the Lord wanted the semen to dry up in the loins of man, He would not have made the procreation of the child, His image, depend upon it, bringing with the act a feeling of supreme satisfaction and fulfillment. The Jewish woman Miriam, or Mary, who immaculately bore the Lord's only begotten son, was the wife of the Jew Joseph, whose semen she took to bear him four more children; and there was no sin in Mary, and no sin in Joseph.

I wonder whether the heavens would frown, if the millions of young men and women who have subjected themselves to unnatural and ungodly vows of abstinence were to come back to us, and join the families of the world and live as the Lord designed them to live?

Abstinence has made no one happy, but has brought sorrow to many folk. There is no Sodomism in man's living with woman. Adam lived a long time alone in Eden, quite alone, until the Lord smiled and gave him Eve. And from that day on, there isn't a single word to be found in the Scriptures coming from the Lord telling man to cast Eve out from his tent or hide out alone in a desert cave.

# Biology and Biography

RARELY HAS A GOOD BIOGRAPHY BEEN WRITTEN OF A living person—boy, man, or senex; and as for biographies about those who have crossed the Styx, it is not too difficult for an imaginative writer—let us call him ghost writer—to let the ghost tamper with the truth, creating a fanciful portrait bearing historical implications and anecdotal riches that had reality only in the clever head of the man with the facile pen.

How much does one know about the man living next door? A cursory inspection of criminological records will establish that some of the most fiendish crimes were committed by persons who outwardly led a most exemplary life; and let us not overlook the fact that the number of crimes never uncovered is far greater than those that are brought to justice.

By the same token, a man who is spending his life behind the bars of a penal institution—brought there as an adolescent by one of the many twists of fate, perhaps for being lookout for a gang of juvenile delinquents staging an armed robbery, without his even realizing the nature and gravity of his participation—such a man may carry in his heart more goodness and uprightness than many of the people outside the drab confines of his jail.

What does one really know about what moves a person, and to what he is moved, who has not experienced in his own life, when fate's pendulum swung the other way, how close friends became strangers and even antagonists, and how neglected and distant people came close, stretching out a helping hand. We joke and cartoon about the obviousness of "being nice to the rich uncle," but I for one would rather laugh at the relative who is rude to the rich and kind to the impoverished.

Such are the difficulties that writing a biography entails. The act itself in the light of history is secondary. It is the motive that matters. Tell me your motives, and I will tell you what you are—but who shows his motives? Like the Chinese women of old who carefully covered their feet, people hide their driving power, showing only the surface of their deeds. In times of mass prejudice or psychotic persecutions, how many have the urge to help sudden victims when they are running for cover, how many resist the temptation and advantages of running with the hunter instead of the hunted?

Perhaps this is the greatest difference between man and man, far greater than the differences in pigmentation, in ancestry, and even education: where there are stronger, do you join the weaker?

How is a biographer to tell what impelled a man towards a certain action. The most nefarious movements have frequently had a most angelic ideological front. Hitler ranted like a medieval mystic, Mussolini like a travel bureau version of Caesar, and Tojo like an Asia-struck Shinto priest.

And at the bottom of these three black hearts there was nothing but a swilly greed to get on top of this world, with all the takings for themselves and their henchmen, and not a care for the rest of the world.

Still some biographers drew some pretty portraits of these three blackguards.

The biographer is like the man who longs to see the legendary lady in the castle window. She raises the blinds only when she is ready for you, all made up and dressed up and smiled up. From afar, you can scarcely tell whether she is 17 or 70, and when you take a second look the blinds come down.

# The Arts and the Nothing

ART DENOTES A TALENT OF EXPRESSION. FOR LONG
we have divided art into artisanship and creative
art. What, then, is creative art?

Mythology has it that art was born when the
girl Corinthia traced the features of her departing
lover in a shadowy outline on a wall. Taken symbolically, this is perhaps as good a definition of the
origin and essence of art as any. Among ancient
peoples, such as the Sumerians, Babylonians, or
Hittites, we find a respectable amount of accomplished artisanship, but the traces of true art are
rare. Speaking symbolically again, perhaps we can
find, in the Hebrew denial of the artist's right to
choose any other subject but the Lord Himself, a
key to the inner sanctum of *ars artis*.

The despair of Corinthia and her yearning
somehow to create a material form for her departing beloved, the tumultuous impatience of the
ancient Israelites with the gods and goddesses of

old, whom they as well as the other nations had worshipped, and who were tumbling at the prophetic advent of Jehovah, the one and only, the God of their hearts and souls, their lives and conscience, who was to put an end to gods of stone with the heads of eagles and the rumps of lions—these are, in a deep sense, indicative of the depths whence true art rises.

The facile pen, the easy brush, the clever easel—these make not the artist, though they may make the artisan. The author of the Psalms or of *Hamlet*, the painter of Mona Lisa, the sculptor of the Pietà, the composer of the Eroica—they differ less in the manner of their artistry from the many other performers than they do in the depth and scope of their creations. It is that creativity—the call from the beyond—that makes the difference between the shouting artist and the artist of calling.

When one wanders through the eerie galleries of modern exhibitions, looking at the weird forms and nightmares of our surrealistic painters and sculptors and the shrewdly hung abstractions of their contemporaries with uncanny business and publicity sense—one wonders where there is to be found in this uncultivated weed patch even a single blossom of beauty.

*Kalos K'agathos*, the beautiful and the good— there is no other measure of true art. *Agatos* in the Platonic sense is the idea of the *summum bonum* that in the heart of man preaches humanity and deity—the Godly, the Humane, the Beautiful Idea.

Without this idealism, without this inner drive from the depth of man's Self, art was, is, and must remain tinsel deep. This original unity of art and mysticism was known to the sages of all times, and where this unity does not prevail, no true artistic originality can be achieved, notwithstanding all the multiple calculated and fanciful machinations and fabrications of novelty-drunk Dadaists, Cubists, Abstractionists, Surrealists, Futurists and Existentialists. There always have been a great many more or less experienced operators in the arts who have the barker's gift for borrowing the ears of audiences. The fields of music and painting, sculpture and poetry are filled with the persuasive shouts of these pseudos and dilettantes who are cluttering up not only our galleries, music halls and theatres, but even our periodicals and books, with their overbearing mediocrity.

Even if the voices of the truly creative were to drop to a whisper and their sculpture and paintings retained in the attic, the relentless wheel of time will grind the folly of jazzy ceramics and noisy coulages to deserved dust, and the winds of true creativity will blow them thither and unearth *Kalos K'agathos* tomorrow and tomorrow *perennis!*

# Hearsay and Heartsay

KNOWLEDGE, AS WELL AS FOOD, IS CONSUMED IN conglomerate patterns. The burden is upon the mind, as upon the body, to break up, separate, and absorb the essentials. What would become of the body were the stomach to permit entry into the blood stream and tissues of all the chaff and eliminanda that constitute the bulk of the food intake?

For some still little known reason, the separatist powers of the brain stand poor comparison with those of the stomach.

Knowledge, which is the food of the mind, reaches it in multifarious forms of purity, complication and confusion.

How few of us sit down to deliberate meditation on the true nature of our concepts and perceptions.

How do we know that what we know is as we know it, and why?—This simple question applied to almost every bit of our knowledge will give us some amazing insights into our own stock of information, opinions, and confusion. This simple question may convince even many a casual reader that—to present an example—he knows as much or as little about the real workings of an electronic tube or a camera as does the man from Timbuktu who certainly doesn't see them in his parlor.

The Western World talks a lot and sermonizes a lot on the life and teachings of Christ, although all it knows about this 2,000-year-old event is what is related by four chapters and a score of letters published in a little book, the earliest available issue of which was written almost 400 years after the occurrence; that is, hundreds of millions of people are willing to subscribe to the divine origin and divine spirit of a charity-imbued Jewish personage, simply because a swarm of miracle-worshipping Hebrew boatsmen and farmers set down some legends concerning a wonder-working rabbi. It is not surprising that in other countries such as India, China, Arabia, and so on, different legends were created of other religious characters together with religious knowledge of a different but frequently no less superficial caliber.

Even a small amount of serious introspection

will show how much of our alleged knowledge is built upon the crumbling foundation of Hearsay.

Some theologians argue cleverly, "One must have faith to understand," but this type of putting-the-cart-before-the-horse logic is practiced by all the faiths that exclude each other with as much vehemence as their living together on the same globe can permit.

Lifting oneself, for the sake of this argument, just a wee bit off this globe, one cannot very well accept Mohammed's dialogues with the angel Gabriel, and the reports of the bodily resurrection of Jesus as well as His Mother, and also the millionfold incarnations and reincarnations of the Hindu believers whose souls, they faithfully maintain, incarnate themselves into cows and kings, beggars, snakes and crocodiles.

Most people who accept one religion on faith pay little heed to the embarrassing situation that a thousand miles across the mountains or the waters people hold with equal firmness to another faith that considers theirs a sham and farce.

Our globe is crisscrossed with faiths and beliefs that are asserted by their adherents to be God inspired and true, infallible in eternal verity. But to us, who at this moment are a wee bit off the globe, it is quite clear and obvious that they can't all be true and still be of verity. Perhaps none of them are true, and they are all just another set of mythologies and legends, some of which have died, as did those of the ancient Greeks or Sumerians or Carthaginians, and some of which are still alive.

Ask yourself what weight there is to your religious knowledge, and remember that faith without knowledge is the apology of the superstitious, the charlatans and the Voodooists.

# The Jealous, the Envious
# and the Fisheyed

JEALOUSY, IN CONTRAST TO ENVY, IS NOTHING BUT
the desire for exclusive possession. In this sense,
and so far as it does not deprive others of something justly due them, it is neither good nor bad,
but rather the expression of a strong feeling of
wanting.

Envy, on the other hand, indicates not so much
the feeling of wanting, as it does the begrudging
of a fellow man's enjoyment of his possessions.
In that sense it represents a negativistic, low-
minded attitude.

Jealousy, or the desire for exclusive possession,
is an emotion frequently confused with the inferiority feeling of the envious. In some respects,
jealousy, if it is lacking, may indicate abnormal
or even perverse tendencies. If Kant's definition of
marriage, which he defined as a mutual agreement of sexual exclusiveness, describes matrimony
correctly, then men and women are justified in

catering to their jealousies, their feelings of exclusive possession. There are men and women in our society who tolerate promiscuity in their mates and even encourage it. But who would describe such a lack of jealousy as anything but a perversion of human emotions?

While jealousy in itself is not only a tolerable, but frequently a desirable attitude, it may occasionally give rise to suspicions which are embarrassing and annoying. But we can as little negate the justification of jealousy because it may create incidental attitudes such as suspicion, as we can approve jealousy's counterpart, envy, because it may occasionally be the direct cause of enterprise, diligence, even philanthropy.

The man who loves a woman would want her for himself; it is only natural for him to desire that all her feminine affections be concentrated on himself. She might therefore assume that a lack of such wanting for exclusive possession is less indicative of a lofty humanitarian feeling than it is of a simple lack of wanting. In a sense, jealousy is the measure of love. Those who don't love are scarcely ever jealous, although they may occasionally be envious.

Not only in sexual relations is love the fundament of jealousy. In friendship, even in the relation of parent to child, the rule holds true: There is no jealousy only where love is neither lost nor gained.

Father and mother want their children to grow according to a pattern they have set for them. The parents may identify themselves with this pattern either in reality or in their day-dreams, and jealously they guard the affections of their offspring lest these affections stray to persons alien to them. Here, too, we may find parents who are not jealous of the affections of their children, who are even indifferent. There are parents who are willing, even glad, to have their children raised in a life away from themselves emotionally as well as physically. Such parents would scarcely be singed by the flames of jealousy. Where there is no fire, one cannot be burned; where there is no love, there can be no jealousy. The parent who does not care whether his children are raised, grow up, and live a thousand miles from his own life, has little love for them, for love wants communion and union. This being together is the one determining goal of love. Lovers want to be together, may they be man and woman or mother and daughter, or just two pals. Lovers want to love and to be loved in return. The deeper the love, the stronger is the desire for exclusiveness and togetherness. And therefrom springs the flame of jealousy.

And where aloofness exists, together with indifference toward living continents apart, founded upon a cold theoretical sense of belonging, naturally there is scarcely a trace of jealousy.

It is to be expected that cold and unconcerned groups would dislike and avoid the emotional heat that comes with jealousy. But beneath the sting and the sparks of this peculiar blaze there lies an ever-burning hearth of human affection—of wanting to be together, undisturbed, with one's loved ones, in this brief interlude of man's global journey.

# Fame Wearies the Hunter

FAME IS THE BITTER FRUIT ON A THORNY MOUNTAIN bush, shining lusciously to those watching from afar; but to the climbers who partake of it, the taste is ashen. Fame does not nourish the soul of man; it wearies the hunter and in the end he becomes the victim of the chase.

Fame spreads in the grasping arms of turbulent man until all the strength and time and breath inherent to mortals are spent in the embrace of the clothed chimera, and man is left nothing but a stumbling shadow of his true self.

Fame cannot be possessed. It cannot even be arrested, and if some naive ambitious hold it for their own, let them only take one further look, to find how precarious is their footing.

Fame is that magic box plant, its roots in the shallowness of public acclaim, its stem and leaves at the whim of plebeian moods. Even some of the truly great have not been spared its acridity. How true are the words of Rabbi Hillel: "A name made great is a name destroyed."

If we take as true the words of Rabban Simeon, the son of the great Gamaliel, that the world is resting on three things only: on truth, on peace, and on justice, then the greed for personal fame serves none of the three. It seems as blessing to those touched by the titillations of a novelty-hungry audience. But some discover early, some later or much too late, that once in the arena there is no rest from clowning, and pretense must go on if the glory-bewitched wants to hold the fluttering attention of the amusement-eyed gallery. No good or God is served by the fame-bound. And those who worry as to what their public will think have only belated concern as to truth and justice and peace.

# The Heinzelmaennchen
## of Psychology

DREAMS ARE BUT THE DROWSY TOSSING OF THE
mind on its retiring into sleep, or on its waking
from sleep. As the mind is slowly shut against the
many senses, five of which we choose to classify,
the last memories and the last sense impressions
play a strong part in the toylandish flights of the
dreamer's fancy, and from the endless treasury of
our memories bizarre and fantastic patterns of
association will hop out, chasing the *Heinzelmaennchen* of yesternight's dreams and tomorrow's illusions. There is no more to these webs of
drowsiness, excepting that, as any one can experi-
ment on himself, a heavy meal of meat and liquor
in the company of coarse men or women will draw
a different brand of morphium over us than an
evening spent in study with one of the Saints, with
milk and crackers for supper.

There is a whole science of how to influence

dreams, known to the concoctors of drugs as well as to men of more gentle purpose. The bed you lie on, the humidity and temperature of your room, the fact that you sleep alone or in company, the familiarity of your nightly surroundings or the strangeness of them—these as well as the factors mentioned before form the net on which the dreams toss in the night.

To give those *Walpurgis-nacht* and sandman's festivals weighty interpretations or secret meanings is as valid a form of scientific research as the erudite dream interpretations of the Babylonian priests, the gypsy nannys of the'pusta, or those of the aborigine tribes of the Philippines who claim that the spirits of the deceased are the true makers of the dreams.

# Syntax and Sense

LANGUAGE, LIKE ANY OTHER FORM OF HUMAN activity, operates in two ways. It is either an imitation of existing patterns, following tradition and mode, or, language may become the expression of an autochthonous thought process. In this latter case, the human mind, using some of the existing language patterns, creates in its search for reality and truth language of its own, be it prose or poetry. Here again, we find only few men or women who are truly linguistically creative.

Most of our other literature, as well as conversation, follows word stereotypes without a trace of true originality.

Certainly, the most intricate and pretty patterns can be woven in traditional syntax. Text may be flowery, paragraphs may be bristling with words put together cunningly, poetry may become startling with abstractions thrown off without sense or meaning, like the sticks of runes of ancient Europe giving off crazy patterns when falling to the ground. Here we have modernistic poetry and glittering prose, fiction and non-fiction alike. But with all this word involvement and word glitter, this type of literature is bereft of basic thought, like a bouquet of paper flowers.

Real language in depth is created by real thought in depth. The real searchers of the human mind and the human soul are the real creators of great literature. And one monologue of the Great Bard, the greatest of them all, is worth a thousand sparkling pages of Hauptmann pretense.

Language makes not the man; it is the man who makes language. Perhaps our schools would do better to guide the young in a search for the truer thought, the deeper concept, instead of a better syntax.

# Death Is Not a Sudden Guest

SLEEP HAS OFTEN BEEN REFERRED TO AS THE brother of death. This is not so at all; sleep is the brother of life.

During our "being awake" we are in a continuous process of dying. As early as adolescence, youth is under the seal of death. As we walk and work, as we play and eat, our intricate machinery is consuming its parts. Death is not a sudden guest; he walks with us all the days of our life, through all the stages of our "being awake"; he leaves us only when we fall into sleep. Every night of natural sleep is a return to the womb of the mother, whence we wake with new life. Without sleep, life's great repairman, our bodies and minds would deteriorate rapidly.

Sleep is the great mender of damage to body and mind. Open your arms to sleep, not only at night, when your exhausted body drops into it habitually or reluctantly—open your arms to sleep when you are hurt, no matter where or why, and entrust yourself to life's very brother, sleep.

# The Nobodies and the Somebodies

SNOBBERY IS THE INSOLENT ATTITUDE ADOPTED BY Nobodies against the indifference of the world of Somebodies. The Somebodies, in carrying on the tasks of real life, have neither time nor taste for petty pretense. The man who has done a day's work sits down to the table and partakes of his food in a manner most in keeping with his hunger and thirst. The snob, having spent hours in the boring venture of killing time, on sitting down cogitates the possibility of creating out of the mundane business of eating and drinking some type of activity that will render him distinct from the common man.

Snobbery is quite an ancient form of effrontery, and long ago the man of small caliber created a rather intricate system of dining, the mastering of which he considered a major accomplishment, justifying not merely his existence *per se*, but putting his existence on a level exalted above that of the ordinary man. It is natural that the ambition of the snob should reach beyond the subtleties of dining. Self-justification is a dynamic force and a snob's attitude spreads from dining to dressing. To him the man who knows not the distinction between black and white tie is as boorish as the fellow who walks downstairs in front of a lady instead of in back of her.

All these minor expressions of snobbery, including the sporting of a monocle, are symptomatic of an immature mind that cannot comprehend the larger issues of life, being thoroughly convinced that the hundred pebbles in his path are life's milestones.

The officer's spouse who would not admit enlisted men's wives to share the swimming pool, although the latter, from anybody's but a snob's point of view might be infinitely better persons; the paper-lipped matron hailing from *Mayflower* immigrants, who would not invite the alien's wife to her dinner party because his ship was of more recent registry—as if she didn't know that there were more criminals and derelicts on the Mayflower than on any boat crossing the Atlantic today; the liquor salesman who would not live in the same house with a Chinese because of his

Asiatic ancestry, although the antecedents of the Chinese were probably putting poetry to the brush while the salesman's ancestors were still sharing their cave with the cattle—all try to conceal their shortcomings under the insolence of snobbery.

Snobbery is an attitude of infantile forgetfulness—forgetfulness that in this fleeting ocean of life all these man-made distinctions born of petty desire, created by smallish minds, are mere pebbles over which the water-mountains float endlessly, majestically. The Somebodies of the world live in awareness of the *panta rei* (the all-flowing) and look with indifference upon the snobbish markers set up by the children of arrogance.

You can't pull rank on God and no man walks past Saint Peter's gate with a monocle in his face.

# Index

# INDEX

cross, 138
Cubists, 162

Dadaists, 162
da Vinci, Leonardo, 87
death, 18, 178
democracy, 129
"deus," 6
Disraeli, 63
divinity, 18, 27
dreams, 175

Eden, 155
education, 78
Egypt, 74, 130, 136
ens eterna, 104
Envy, 168
Epictetus, 152
Essenes, 151
ethics, 22, 115
Europe, 5, 11, 38, 45, 71, 75, 78, 97, 115, 119, 126, 135, 138
Eve, 155
Existentialists, 162

faith, 166
Falstaff, 137
Fascism, 79
Father, the, 137
Faust, 55
fertilizer, 24
France, 39
Frederick the Great, 71
freedom, 125
friendship, 50
Fries, 139
Futurists, 162

Gabriel, 166
Galilei, Galileo, 20

Gamaliel, 173
Gandhi, 117, **151**
Gehenna, 30
"gentlemen's agreement," 105
Georgia, 35, 89
German, 11, 24, 55, 62, 68, 70, 73, 78, 80, 115, 122, 124, 132, 134, 139
ghetto, 75
Gobineau, 71
God, Son of, 137
Greece, 6, 14, 22, 27, 38, 60, 112, 129, 167

Hauptmann, 177
hearsay, 166
Hebrew, 6, 16, 33, 38, 42, 53, 67, 72, 75, 93, 113, 115, 119, 129, 165
Heinzelmaennchen, 174
hell, 30
heritage, racial, 138
Hillel, Rabbi, 83, 173
Hindu, 66, 114, 117, 143, 151, 153, 166
history, 95, 98
Hitler, 12, 52, 54, 79, 122, 130, 144, 158
Hittites, 27, 160
holiness, 118
Holy Ghost, 68, 76
honeymoons, 118
Humility, 103
Huns, 138
Hyksos, 72

Incas, 129
India, 22, 44, 165
Indians, 28
inferiority, 133
intellect, creative, 7
Interference, divine, 12

# INDEX

# INDEX